RENEWALS

REFRESHING AND RESTORING OUR LIVES

Daily Meditations for June and July

Phil Needham

CREST BOOKS

Copyright © 2023 by The Salvation Army

Published by Crest Books

Crest Books
The Salvation Army National Headquarters
615 Slaters Lane
Alexandria, VA 22314
Phone: 703-684-5523

Major Jamie Satterlee, *Director of Publications*
Maryam Outlaw, *Editorial Assistant*
Staci Williams, *Graphic Designer*

ISBN print: 978-1-946709-11-0

Scripture quotations in this publication are from the Common English Bible. © Copyright 2011 by the Common English Bible. All rights reserved. Used by permission.

All rights reserved. No part of this publication may be reproduced, stored in a retrieval system, or transmitted in any form or by any means without prior written permission of the publisher. Exceptions are brief quotations in printed reviews.

Contents

Introduction to These Meditations 1
How to Take This Journey 7

Weeks 1–2: God Together, We together

June 1: Only One God 11
June 2: The One God, A Perfect Community 14
June 3: The Church, A Trinitarian Community 17
June 4: Love-Based Relationships 20
June 5: The Challenge of Inclusiveness 23
June 6: A Faith Journey in Unity with Others 26
June 7: Oneness 29
June 8: Equality 32
June 9: Friendship 35
June 10: Forgiveness 38
June 11: Fellowship 41
June 12: Humility 44
June 13: Together in Service 47
June 14: Together in Suffering 50

Weeks 3–5: Relational Covenants

OUR PERSONAL COVENANTS 56
June 15: A Covenant of Intimacy 57
June 16: A Covenant of Transparency 60
June 17: A Covenant of Grace 63
June 18: A Covenant of Attentiveness 66
June 19: A Covenant of Obedience 69
June 20: A Covenant of New Revelations 72
June 21: A Covenant of Life Together Forever 75

OUR CHURCH COVENANTS 78
June 22: Joining the Family 79
June 23: Joining the Choir 82
June 24: Loving Each Other 85
June 25: Sharing the Wonder 88
June 26: Being Christ's Bride 91
June 27: Loving the Church 94
June 28: Coming Home to Church 97

OUR WORLD COVENANTS 100
June 29: Allegiance to God's Creation 101
June 30: Allegiance to the Kingdom of God 104
July 1: Allegiance to Ourselves 107
July 2: Allegiance to Our Family 110
July 3: Allegiance to Our Church 113
July 4: Allegiance to Our Nation 116
July 5: Allegiance to the Poor and Outcasts 119

WEEK 6: SUMMER GIFTS

July 6: Holidays and Holy Days 124
July 7: Letting Go and Taking Hold 127
July 8: Restoration and Healing 130
July 9: Solitude 133
July 10: Retreats 136
July 11: Risks 139
July 12: Re-Entry 142

WEEKS 7–9: THE BLESSINGS OF THE BEATITUDES

July 13: Jesus 149
July 14: The Poor in Spirit and the Poor 152
July 15: Those Who Mourn and Weep 155
July 16: The Humble 158

July 17: Those Who Are Hungry and Thirsty for
    Righteousness 161
July 18: Those Who Show Mercy 164
July 19: Those Who Have Pure Hearts 167
July 20: The Peacemakers 170
July 21: Those Who Are Persecuted for Their
    Righteousness 173
July 22: The Insulted and Maligned 176
July 23: Those Who Are Not Scandalized Because of the
    Crucified 179
July 24: Those with Eyes to See and Ears to Hear 182
July 25: Those Who Are Faithful Servants 185
July 26: The Givers 188
July 27: The Open-Table Hosts 191
July 28: The Favored Humble 194
July 29: Those Who Die in the Lord 197
July 30: The Blessed Hope 200
July 31: Those Blessed by the Father, Welcomed
    by Christ 203

ADDENDUM: THE NAME OF THE FIRST PERSON IN THE TRINITY

WORKS CITED

Acknowledgments

As I now complete the fourth book of meditations in this Christian Year series, I again express gratitude and love to my wife Keitha, first, for her continuing patience in honoring the space and time I needed to complete this book; and, second, for her valuable assistance in making both corrections and comments. The corrections were gratefully received. The comments led to helpful clarifications and discussions. We have been a team.

I also want to express my gratitude to Crest Books for encouraging and supporting my writing and to their excellent staff—Major Jamie Satterlee, Maryam Outlaw, Staci Williams, and Andrea Martin—for their valuable guidance and assistance in successfully bringing this book to print.

Above all, I am grateful for this opportunity to employ my inadequate words to honor and praise our more-than-adequate God, and to invite you, the reader, to join me in this exploration of life renewal as followers and imitators of Jesus.

Introduction to These Meditations

These meditations commence a season of the Christian Year that begins in June. The previous seasons were Advent and Christmastide, Lent to Easter Sunday, and Easter to Pentecost. Each of those seasons was marked by significant holy days, church observances, and festivals. Most importantly, they focused on the life of Jesus from his conception and birth to his life and death, followed by his resurrection and ascension.

So, what do we call the last six months of the Christian Year? Good question. The more traditional liturgical churches call this timeframe Trinity, or the Sundays in Trinity, bringing the Year to its conclusion where Advent begins the cycle again. In other words, Trinity takes up the full second half of the Christian Year.

Why call these six months 'Trinity'? The early Christians inherited from the Jewish faith a strong belief in the one God, whom Jesus referred to as his heavenly Father. They also believed that Jesus was himself the incarnate Son of God, the full embodiment of God in human flesh who revealed on earth the very nature of God through his life of sacrificial love. That is why the first six months of the Christian Year focus on his life, ministry, crucifixion, resurrection, and his ascension to the Father. And they conclude with the coming of the Holy Spirit, the third Person of the Trinity. Through this Pentecostal invasion of his Holy Spirit, God gave the young church the gift of pure hearts, freeing and empowering Christians to love and serve, imitating their Lord Jesus.

On the eve of Trinity, the church stood on the cusp of a revolution. God had unleashed his threefold Personhood in the

Divine Father's incomparable love for the world, in the Divine Son's self-giving offering of that love to the world, and in the Holy Spirit's gifting of that love to a people ready to risk their lives for it. The Christian church was birthed, not as an organization but as a Trinitarian Movement, loved by their God in three Persons—Father, Son, and Holy Spirit—undivided in power and glory. The Trinity was the source, expression, and power of the Christian revolution.

Seeing the Trinity in this way opens a door into the heart of God. Over the centuries, Christian theologians have tried to explain the Trinity logically. Too often this has led to debates, disagreements, and divisions. There are some realities that the mind cannot fully grasp, things that we know are true even though they can't be proven by rational argument. We cannot figure out the mind of God (Romans 11:34; 1 Corinthians 2:16), but we can know what is in his heart because he has revealed it to us (1 John 4:7-10). Seeing the love that permeates and commands God's heart sheds light on what he is doing in the world and what he is asking us to let him do in our lives.

In the days to come, we shall explore together how our trinitarian God invites us to partner with him for our sake and for the sake of the world. This invitation helps to explain other names used to designate these final six months in the Christian Calendar. Many Christian denominations call this period Ordinary Time or Common Time—not ordinary in the sense of unimportant and not common in the sense of uninteresting, but rather, ordinary and common in the sense of the issues we deal with day after day. *Everyday* issues. Issues we may have mistakenly come to think are not as relevant to our Christian faith or spiritual practices. Those times when we may even neutralize our Christian values or come to think they are not now "relevant." Times when we go along with whatever behaviors are expected or commonly seen as more "appropriate" for the space we are currently occupying or the situation we find ourselves in.

Perhaps the mentality that has most weakened Christians and undermined the credibility of our witness in the world is our acceptance of the practice of dividing our time between sacred and secular. There are the times when we go to church, have fellowship with other Christians, or have personal devotions. These are the times when we are likely to feel we are in touch with God: *sacred* times. Then there are the times—for most of us, it is by far the greater part of our days—when we are in a world that operates mostly by motivations and goals that are foreign to the values of the kingdom of God. God does not seem near in this world, and we may feel cut off from or unsupported by our faith community. So, we may do what we think we must do to get by, or come out on top, or perhaps just lay low so that our Christian values will not be put to the test. These are *secular* times.

If we separate sacred times from secular times, we are abandoning our calling as Christians. The separation is pagan. All of life is the arena of God. All venues of our lives are places where the love of God is waiting to stake a claim. We are there for a divine reason, and the reason—in whatever shape or form it manifests itself, or however awkward or clumsy our effort to respond to it are—is to embody the love of God. How else can we believe and credibly live out John 3:16? Whichever part of the world we are occupying and whoever is present at the time, the reality is that God is there loving it and them. Probably not approving of things as they are, but wanting us to play some role in revealing the ways he is trying to break through. Behind

RENEWALS

the so-called secularity of our days, God is present, his love is at work, and in one way or another, we are called to be his heart and his hands, however we do it.

We are not alone in this calling. We have the God who gifts us with his love, who came to earth as one of us to authenticate this love through crucifixion, and whose Spirit is present with us, opening our hearts and showing us the way to welcome him into all the moments of our days, making our ordinary days extraordinary. God has also gifted us with the church, the Body of Christ, our support system—our place of worship, guidance, and nurturing. When we live our lives in the world, we bring our support system with us as we pray for one another. When we leave church, we take the church with us. We are never alone.

For these reasons, my meditations will seek to be as comprehensive and inclusive as possible of the kinds of opportunities and challenges we meet in our private lives, the lives of our church, and our lives in the world. They will require us to think and pray through tough issues with some depth in all three areas. God always—yes, *always*—has work to do in all three areas, and we are privileged to have his presence and guidance when we are willing to abandon the illusion of our self-sufficiency and follow the ways and means of his love. My prayer is that these meditations will be helpful to that end.

(Note: The Trinity/Common/Ordinary Time books of daily meditations will be divided into three books. The first (this book) will be meditations for the early summer season (June-July); the second, for the late summer and early fall season (August-September); and the third, for late fall and early winter (October-November). Unlike the previous meditations, we will strictly follow the dates of the secular calendar, beginning June

1 and concluding July 31; then August 1, concluding September 30; and finally, October 1, concluding November 26.)

*****

I'd like to explain my reason for giving this first book of the June–November series the title, *Renewals: Refreshing and Restoring Our Lives*. Summer seems to be a time of the year that lends itself not only to relaxation and fun, but also to some form of rejuvenation. We don't feel as rushed. Our schedule may be less rigid, with more open spaces to reassess the way we are living—or who we are living for. We may take more time to reflect, to examine our lives, to think more deeply of our relationships, even to contemplate what our future will be. So, summer is a good time for renewal, a time to refresh and restore our lives.

In this book of meditations, we will seek this renewal by looking at how our God who is Father, Son, and Holy Spirit, a community of Three-in-One, teaches us to pattern our living in all our relationships. In a day when so many feel alienated from God, alone in the world, and without a community of faith or uncomfortable in the one they belong to, this is good news!

During the first two weeks, we will explore how the Trinity draws us into relationships and communities where we reflect the character and grace of God. The third, fourth and fifth weeks will deal with covenants. Every real community is based on a covenant of some kind, whether it is in writing or implied. We will look at our personal covenants, our church covenants, and our covenants with the world in which God has placed us as witnesses. The sixth week will consider the spiritual value of some of the special gifts of the summer season. Weeks seven, eight, and the first five days of week nine will focus on the Beatitudes

RENEWALS

as laying before us how Jesus invites us to live our common, everyday lives in ways that mirror the love, graces, and blessedness of eternity.

How to Take This Journey

There are three parts to each meditation. The first includes suggested Scripture passages for reflection in preparation for the meditation. They relate to the subject of the meditation, though they may not be specifically referenced in the meditation itself. I suggest you read these passages first, maybe even offer a prayer the words call you to. The second part is the meditation itself, which is designed to stimulate and challenge your own reflection around the subject of the meditation. The third part is a concluding prayer, shaped by the Scripture and the meditation, which you are invited to pray for yourself. You may want to add to the prayer or pray in your own words.

It is important that this time of meditation take place in a controlled setting where interruptions are less likely to distract you. For many, that time would be in the early morning. For others for whom private space is next to impossible at that time of day, other arrangements can be made.

Although the meditations are designed for your personal devotions, it may be desirable for a very small group—for example, a married couple or a group of friends—to do the devotions together, followed by a time of sharing. Two to four people could do them together through a scheduled conference call or virtual meeting each day. Perhaps a group of people who are doing the meditation alone could meet, do a conference call, or access a virtual meeting once a week and share what the week's journey has meant to them, then pray together for each other. Please use these meditations in a way that best meets your needs.

WEEKS 1–2
GOD TOGETHER, WE TOGETHER

For many Christians, the doctrine of the Trinity is a puzzle. Maybe it is for you as well. You probably believe in it, but when it gets down to trying to explain it logically, you struggle. You may over-emphasize the individuality of each of the three Persons so much that you end up with three separate gods. Or you may over-emphasize the oneness of God so much that the distinctiveness of the three Persons is lost. They become no more than three sides of God's personality.

Let's face it: The Trinity boggles our minds. But that is not a bad thing. A few years ago, T. M. Luhrmann, a professor of anthropology at Stanford University, wrote a column based on a concept introduced by historian Renee Haynes called "boggle threshold." He took the idea and applied it to his own work as a scientist. Science reaches a point at which the ways scientists have been conditioned to think do not allow them to accept certain things. This does not mean those things are not true. It only means current science can't prove they are true. They boggle our limited ways of thinking. Often, those boggles prove to be true, helping us to see in new and better ways. Luhrmann goes on to suggest that faith is something like that. Hebrews 11:1 tells us that "faith is the reality of what we hope for, the proof of what we don't see." To have faith is to allow our minds to be boggled by something that cannot be rationally proven, but we sense or perceive that there is a deeper reality to it, something we can't avoid, truth that opens doors to life.

The Trinity is a boggle. We can't define it; it defines *us*. It is beyond our thinking; it thinks us. In fact, it is not an 'it'; it is three Persons in one God. And this God who is Father, Son, and Holy Spirit holds the life secret of what it means for us to be created in his image, which is what it means to be human.

The meditations for these first two weeks will look at what it means for us to be created in the image of the God who is both One and Three, and how this image shapes the way we live our lives in the time we have on earth. We will explore how the life and love of the Trinity permeates the life and love of the church, the Body of Christ on earth. We will:

- Explore the oneness and the three-ness of God, and how this unity-in-diversity is the way divine love operates.
- Consider how the love-based relationships within the Trinity create a love-based church that is inclusive and where members move forward together in unity.
- Explore how the oneness of the Trinity is reflected in the unity of church members and in their partnership together on their faith journey.
- See the influence that the oneness and the equality of the three Persons has on the unity and mutual respect of fellow members of the Body of Christ.
- Discover the importance of treating fellow church members as friends with whom we share deep fellowship and the gifts of confession and forgiveness.
- See our calling to humble ourselves before one another, serve others together, and support one another in our suffering with and for Christ.

Note: For those who are interested, a further discussion of naming the first Person of the Trinity the 'Father' is available as an addendum in the back of this book.

JUNE 1
ONLY ONE GOD

Scripture for Reflection: Deuteronomy 6:4-6; Ephesians 4:5-6

One of the most important declarations of faith for both Jews and Christians is found in the Deuteronomy passage above. It's usually referred to by the opening word in Hebrew, *Shema* ('Hear!' or 'Listen!' in English), making what follows sound like a wake-up call, a summons to what is most essential, something that must be taken seriously. What follows is, in fact, all that and more: "Israel, listen! Our God is the Lord! Only the Lord!" The passage has been rendered in different ways by various translators, but the message is the same: We have only one God (v.4) who merits being loved by us with all our heart, being, and strength (v.5) Always remember this! (v.6).

In the day, the *Shema* was a revolutionary statement. Polytheism, the worship of multiple gods, characterized most if not all other religions. If you have multiple gods, each of those gods serves a different purpose for you. You go to the god that you believe can give you what you need or want at the time. But you know that this god first demands something from you, typically a sacrificial offering of some kind. In other words, your relationship with that god is *transactional*. Presumably, both sides get something from the transaction, very much like the practical ways we get along in day-to-day business.

The *Shema* forbids us to deal with God in that way. God does not want payment for services; he wants us to love him for who he is, in every way (v.5), without expecting favors. If we ask *why* he wants us to love him, the answer lies in who he is and who we are in his image. He *is* love, and the only way to get to know him is to love him in return. He is the divine Lover, and we are the creations of his love, privileged to remain in his love, and free to return it (see 1 John 4:7-8, 16-17).

What about other gods? Well, they don't exist. They are human creations who become real only in our hearts and lives because they serve our self-serving purposes. They are glorifications of our own pursuits, projections of our private wishes, embodiments of our self-serving drives. They are *our* creations, and we give them a life of their own, which they would not otherwise have.

God is not *only* One; he is the only One. Paul puts it in his letter to the Ephesian church this way: "There is one Lord … and one God and Father of all, who is over all, through all, and in all" (Ephesians 4:5-6).

If you are a follower of Jesus, it is easy to agree that our God is our One and Only. There are two ways for us to test our claim. The first is for us to immerse ourselves in Scripture and good spiritual direction and ask the Spirit to give us understanding of what God's love is calling us to and asking of us. We too easily assume that we know the answers. Often, we don't. In fact, we may well have false information. It is the nature of Scripture to constantly challenge our assumptions of what it means to follow the One and Only God.

The second way for us to test ourselves is to take honest looks at who we are really following and what is motivating us as we live our lives in the world. Under the Spirit's influence we may come to see that we are following the gods of materialism, promotion, prominence, or power, for example. We may have learned, however, to frame these gods in nice, socially acceptable ways, and have even come to see success in these pursuits as God's blessing. We may have failed to test the moral fiber of our motivations.

There is only one God, and his name is Love. You and I are called to answer his incredible love with our love and to live in a way that releases his love into the world.

Dear God, who is love, turn my heart more and more in the direction of the One and Only God. Help me to see you as you are, obey you as you wish, and be guided as you choose. I ask this in the name of Jesus, Son of You, the One and Only God, who alone deserves to have my worship, my praise, and my life. Amen.

JUNE 2

THE ONE GOD, A PERFECT COMMUNITY

Scripture for Reflection: 2 Corinthians 13:13; Ephesians 3:14-19

Yesterday, we considered the biblical witness that God is One and there is only one God. Today, we take a closer look at God's oneness. Oneness may sound unimaginative. God's oneness, however, is anything but boring. It is a dynamic Trinity.

The writers of the New Testament did not inherit a formal doctrine of the Trinity, although there are passages in the Old Testament that hint of a diversity in God (for example, Genesis 18:1-15). In the Gospels, we find Jesus, the incarnate Son of God, praying to his heavenly Father at the beginning of his ministry and all the way to the final hours of his earthly life. The Book of Acts records appearances of the Holy Spirit of God to and in the church. The final verse of Paul's second letter to the Corinthian church brings this threefold-ness of God together in a beautiful benediction: "The grace of the Lord Jesus Christ, the love of God, and the fellowship of the Holy Spirit be with you all." We get the sense that, at the very least, the givers of divine grace, love, and fellowship are a close partnership. Paul's letter to the Ephesian church (3:14-21) reveals an even more detailed description of how Father, Son (Christ), and Holy Spirit work together in the life of the church or a congregation. So, how do we see the relationship between the Three?

Let's return to something I said in the introduction to this first week of Trinity. I said that the Trinity is a boggle. It boggles our minds. This does not mean it makes no sense or that it is a fiction, nor that it should be dismissed. On the contrary, it should be embraced precisely because when we explore it, we are led into the depths of God, the mystery that is truth beyond our limited rational thinking. If we try to describe it conceptionally, however, we are left with dry dogma that stays imprisoned in our minds—a cerebral Trinity, devoid of life and love.

How, then, do we describe the Trinity? We describe it as three Persons in loving unity with each other—each one lending their unique gifts to the other for the life of the one God and the salvation of the whole world. The One and Only God is a community of three who work together in concert, each Person loving, supporting, and facilitating the other. The Trinity is not three Persons "doing their own thing." They are one. And because God is love, they are united in love with one another. As I once heard Salvation Army officer Bill Ury sum it up, they "give themselves to one another." And in one form or another, they work together to release the overflow of God's love into the world. In other words, think of the Trinity as a perfect community of love—love both for each other and for the world.

Why is this important for us? It is important because it gives us the vision of the kind of community our church is called to be as the Body of Christ. As the three Persons of the Trinity work together in love, so our church is called to work together in love. As each of the three Persons brings unique contributions to the work of God, so are we each, as members of the Body, called to bring our respective gifts as needed offerings to the ministry and the mission of the church. As the three Persons humble themselves before each other, so must we if we are to be and to look like the Body of Christ.

In future meditations, we will explore the practical meanings of the Trinity for the character and life of the church. As we do so, I invite you to consider and pray about how your own church community can grow in grace together. After all, we are called to live our lives as those who have been created in the image of God. As we discover who we are together, we will more and more reflect the life and love of the Trinity.

> *Lord of love, free me from the sin of building myself up. Give me the humility to count others better than myself and to partner with others for the sake of your Body of Christ and the salvation of the world. I ask this in your name and for the sake of your church. Amen.*

June 3
The Church, a Trinitarian Community
Scripture for Reflection: 1 John 4:7-21

In the early years of my life as a Christian, my church taught me basic Christian doctrines. This teaching included the Trinity. I was taught that it was an important way of seeing God at work, but I couldn't quite get my head around 'three Persons in the Godhead.' How could one God be three Persons and three Persons one God? I suspected that there was truth to protect in this doctrine, but I had little idea of how it might relate to my understanding of the church.

At the time, I saw most churches as gatherings of the like-minded—people with similar backgrounds who liked many of the same things and shared the same attitudes, values, and practices. Like a club. "You can join if you fit in with our culture." In time, I learned that the New Testament church was threatened by a similar kind of insularity. It came in the form of Jewish Christians wanting only Gentile converts who were willing to follow strict Jewish laws and practices. The apostle Paul, a converted Jew himself, would have none of it. He took a huge risk in saying that in Christ, Gentile converts were under no such obligations (Ephesians 2:14-16).

This was the beginning of my understanding that the church of Jesus is not an exclusive religious club at all. If it were, most people probably wouldn't meet all the qualifications to be members. They might be turned down because of their ethnicity or race, their economic status, their physical or mental health, their embarrassing personality or social awkwardness, or even their theology. Unfortunately, many—if not most—congregations tend to aim at recruiting new members that they will be comfortable around. People like themselves. But I was now hearing God say also—and especially—to recruit members *not* like us.

In time, I came to see church as a group of people called together to be shaped into the likeness to God: a trinitarian community, a body of people created and redeemed in the image of God, who is Trinity. She is the community of those who are redeemed by Christ, formed by the Spirit, and gathered as one Body to live in eternal praise and witness to their trinitarian God. Ministry within the Body and mission in the world then flow out of this dynamic union.

The Trinity of Father, Son, and Holy Spirit form a perfect union that we call one God. The Bible uses different ways to describe what God is like. Some of these are: faithful, powerful, good, all-knowing, kind. Other words are used to describe who God is in terms of what he does. Some of these are: Creator, Savior, Sanctifier. When it comes to the one word that says who and what God *is*, the word that jumps out and embraces us, wins us, and claims us is: LOVE. It is not enough to say that God is 'loving' or that he 'loves.' Breaking through all the qualifications of language, the apostle John throws down the gauntlet of the Godhead and says, **"God IS love!"** (1 John 4:16b, emphasis added). Not just a God who practices love, as we do some of the time. He *is* love. He defines love. He is the source of it, because he is a perfect community of Father, Son, and Holy

Spirit. There is no love where there is no community, and the Trinity is the community of consummate love.

When we join a church, we are expanding ourselves by limiting ourselves. We are entering the boundaries of a group that takes away our convenient boundaries. The church is God's community on earth, patterned after the inclusive Trinity. As we explore this truth in meditations to follow, apply them to yourself and to the church you are a part of. In what ways are you called to be part of the visible Body of Christ in the unity of Father, Son, and Holy Spirit?

Father, Son, and Holy Spirit, take away my sinful self-centeredness and my fear-based exclusion of those who are not like me. May I, in your strength and by my own example, be a voice in my church for a love-based, inclusive community. I pray in your name. Amen.

JUNE 4

LOVE-BASED RELATIONSHIPS

Scripture for Reflection: Philippians 2:1-5

In the first meditation (June 1), I said that God, our Creator and Redeemer, is love. All true love draws from the mutual love of Father, Son, and Holy Spirit. Redeemed in his image, we cannot escape love. Love defines our relationships; it makes us human in God's image. Do we sometimes fail as God-redeemed lovers? Yes. (Or am I the only one?)

How, then, do we grow in likeness to God as credible reflectors of his image? How do we continue to get better at it? God has given us the answer to that question: *the church*. As we saw earlier, the church is called to live under the sovereignty of the Father, follow the lordship of Christ the Son, and find the unity of love in the Holy Spirit (Ephesians 4:1-6). Hebrews 13:1 instructs church members to "keep loving each other like family." Paul, with obviously deep feeling, describes congregations he founded as "love letters written not with ink but with the Spirit of the living God ... on tablets of human hearts" (2 Corinthians 3:1-3).

We have the perfect model for this love: Jesus of Nazareth. Jesus came as the incarnate Son of God to show us what it is to live God's love on earth. We see it time and again in how he treated people. I'm not saying he was sweet and nice all the time. When faced with Pharisees' superiority and judgment, his love took the form of bold confrontation; with deceivers, uncomfortable truth; with exploiters of others, angry judgment. But with the confused, his love took the form of penetrating clarity; with the hurting, liberating healing; with the seekers, an open door to life in the world of God's love, which he called the kingdom of God.

It would have been convenient if Jesus' teaching of God's love-based kingdom and the extraordinary way his life embodied it had been all that was needed to bring us around. But our fallen nature stood in the way of our following his teaching and the example of his life. In our hearts, we were in rebellion against his love. We preferred to pursue our own "salvations," which took the form of clever schemes for self-enhancement, protection, advancement, and power. Schemes that, in the final analysis, served only us. We were willing to make some "concessions" to God if he let us adapt his love to our advantage. But God doesn't make deals.

The outcome of God's refusal to compromise his love was the Cross. Crucifixion was inevitable, given the supreme integrity of Jesus' self-giving life and the depth of his love for us. The paradox is that the tables were completely turned: suffering love saves. Love willing to surrender its life and suffer horrible death for the ones loved—*all of us*—is saving love.

How do receive this incredible gift? With profound, heart-felt gratitude. What else must we then do? We must work on our relationships and ask the Spirit's help in making them love-based. Love-based in the way of Jesus' self-giving, reflecting trinitarian love in our love for others.

It begins with the church, the Body of Christ, God's gift as the training ground for living out love-based relationships. Churches

RENEWALS

exist for more than camaraderie. They exist for bearing one another's burdens, suffering together, rejoicing together, lifting one another up in prayer. They exist as the reflection on earth of God's kingdom, a convincing expression of trinitarian love.

I invite you to reflect on how you and your congregation can take steps better to become such a community.

Loving Lord, I invite you to teach me God's way of love.
Loving Spirit, I invite you to empower my congregation to be a love-based Body of Christ. I ask in Jesus' name. Amen.

JUNE 5
THE CHALLENGE OF INCLUSIVENESS
Scripture for Reflection: James 2:1-8

In yesterday's meditation I shared my own observation that many—and probably most—church congregations are comprised mostly of people who share a lot in common and are enough alike to be relatively comfortable together. The similarities may relate to race, ethnicity, wealth, or the lack of it, and in some cases rigid or even questionable doctrinal positions that attract some but repulse others. In this meditation we focus on the disparities between what many call 'the Haves and the Have-Nots.' Those who live relatively secure lives and those who don't, those who are well-set, as we say, and those who barely survive from day to day or week to week, whether from lack of necessities or from mental instability.

Many churches donate to programs that help the disadvantaged. Others even have their own ministries to the underserved. My own denomination came into existence specifically to evangelize the oppressed poor and working classes in the slums of Victorian England, but soon realized that this alone was not enough. Caring for the salvation of a person's soul without addressing the horrible social conditions of that person's daily life fell far short of the example of Jesus. The spiritual gospel needed partnering with the social gospel. Early on, the poor and working classes, many of them having received practical help from The Salvation Army, were found in our evangelistic meetings and Sunday morning worship services. What drew them to worship was a religious culture that was far from "high church." It was Christianity recast in the language and music of the working classes, with plenty of personal testimonies thrown in, lending concreteness and credibility to Christ's transformative power.

In our day, perhaps the biggest challenge to a church congregation is to be inclusive of some groups that members are uncomfortable being around. What I mean by inclusive is, yes, serving that group without discrimination, but also going beyond that to finding ways to include them in the life of the church and in the lives of members. To be a recipient of a congregation's social service is helpful; to be welcomed and made to feel at home in the Body of Christ on earth, however, can be transformative—not only for the recipients, but also for the congregation. How that is done depends on a number of factors, including the nature of the need and the particular strengths and capacities of church members. A passion for inclusion, however, is essential.

Peter W. Marty writes about a fourteenth-century church in Geel, Belgium dedicated to Dymphna, the patron saint of the mentally afflicted. According to legend, Dymphna was an Irish princess who fled to Geel to escape her incestuous father. She became known for her personal care for mentally tormented individuals shunned by society. Seven centuries later, families in that small town still take the mentally ill into their homes and call them boarders or guests!

For centuries (says Marty) scholars have been fascinated

by the hospitable attitude of the Geel citizenry toward those with chronic mental illness. Mental differences are routinely accepted; behaviors feared and stigmatized elsewhere are normalized. It's the ultimate community-based model for mental health. A psychiatric hospital in town provides high-level care for those who are violent or experiencing a crisis. Today, nearly 300 boarders live with more than 200 families (CS, January 12, 2022, italics added).

There are many ways Christians and churches can find to be a truly inclusive, Christlike people. What would such inclusion look like for you and your church?

Dear Lord, lover of the poor and outcasts, open my heart to Christ's border-breaking love, my will to the courage to risk it, and my mind to see how. I pray in your name. Amen.

JUNE 6

A FAITH JOURNEY IN UNITY WITH OTHERS

Scripture for Reflection: 1 Corinthians 12:7-27

The dominant religion of our day is not a religion; it is a cult. A cult of our *self*. Self-centeredness is nothing new; it is as old as the Garden of Eden. It seems, however, to have officially become a cult in recent years, enabled by the Internet in the form of selfies and the commentaries that accompany them. Selfies are photos that project our individual selves in different poses, outfits, locations, states of emotion, sometimes taken with different individuals who we hope, in one way or another, enhance or authenticate us. They are attempts to draw and keep others attentive to us. They enable our addiction to ourselves. They are hi-tech's contribution to the cult of self and, for so many, irresistible.

Another more sophisticated version of this cult of our self is found in people, typically younger adults who have severed their connections and ceased their participation in a church. They call themselves SBNRs (spiritual-but-not-religious) because they are not part of a Christian congregation and claim to live by their own personally-crafted version of faith, Christian or otherwise. They usually insist, however, that they are spiritual and have their own religious practices. The reasons they give for their disaffiliation may range from not having their spiritual needs met to having unpleasant experiences in a congregation. Or they may claim that they have observed religion in general as a divisive force in the world. They have come to trust only their own private spirituality. Ironically, studies show that the great majority of the SBNRs do not really have private spiritual practices at all.

A totally private religion can be, in the final analysis, only a cult of one's self. If we're going to build a relationship with God, we're going to have to build a relationship with others who are doing likewise. Let's use a baseball analogy. Pitching a perfect game is one of the great so-called *individual* achievements in baseball. The fact is, it's *never* an individual achievement, because the only way a pitcher can do it is for *at least nine players* to do it, no matter how brilliantly the pitcher has pitched. No one pitches a perfect game unless each teammate has played a perfect game, too. Similarly, one's Christianity only progresses with others who are progressing.

The apostle Paul uses the metaphor of the human body to illustrate what the church is like. No part of the human body can exist without being a working part of the one body. Likewise, no Christian can realize her calling without the love, fellowship, support, nurture, and worship of the Body of Christ, whatever the name by which her particular congregation goes.

Jesus' prayer for his disciples at his last supper with them includes a straightforward prayer for their unity: "I pray they will be one, Father, just as you are in me and I am in you … perfectly one" (John 17:21). We can't miss the message that the church's oneness is enabled by the oneness of the Three-Person God. Jesus then goes on to pray that this unity of his church will enable the world to know that the Father sent Jesus and that he loves the world as he loves Jesus (v. 23b). Bottom line:

RENEWALS

the unity of the church is absolutely key to the credibility and power of its message.

As followers of Christ, we are all on a journey *together*. With the Spirit's help, perhaps you can identify a unifying step that you—with some fellow members—can take now.

Dear God, thank you for creating me to reflect your union as Father, Son, and Holy Spirit. Please teach me how to receive the gift and blessing of this holy unity in fellowship with my brothers and sisters in Christ. I ask this in Jesus' name. Amen.

JUNE 7

Oneness

Scripture for Reflection: John 17:20-23

There is more to say about Jesus' prayer that we, his church, be one as he and the Father are one (John 17:21). It is unity, to be sure, where we live and work together, adding our differences and our diverse giftedness for the common cause of the gospel. But Scripture says we must see, as well, that it is a coming together in a deeper way. It is Christ in each of us seeking after and finding Christ in each other of us. It is the Christ in me seeking, finding, loving, receiving, and learning from the Christ in you. It's not that we each have a different Christ, or a different version of him; it's that, in spite of our obvious differences and disagreements, the Christ in you has something to give me, and the Christ in me something to give you.

When we look for Christ in each other, he may seem hidden. But he is surely there, as he is even and especially in "the least of these" (Matthew 25:40). Followers of Jesus are called to find Jesus in one another, which is a beautiful way to describe how the church lives its life together. Paul tells the church in Rome that even though they are a large, diverse group, they "are one body in Christ, and individually ... belong to each other (Romans 12:5)." This belonging to each other goes beyond membership or even unity. It's not just coming together to unite for a common cause; it is being part of each other—it is a oneness in Christ. Whether we are hearing the voice of Caiaphas (the high priest) or that of John (the author of the Gospel), the prophecy recorded in John 11:52-53 declares that "Jesus would soon die ... not only for the [Jewish] nation ... [but] so that God's children scattered everywhere would be gathered together *as one*. From that day on [the religious authorities] plotted to kill him" (italics added). What was it about that oneness in Christ that was so threatening—and still is?

Deep down, we all know. The Christ in all of us calls us to be more that a cooperative society for him. He calls us to be a family in him. If this sounds warm and cuddly, we need to take a closer look at the battles that had to be fought in the New Testament church to win and then defend the oneness. Once the initial barrier to membership was broken down, the greater challenge emerged. It was the challenge to be a family, not by any blood relations other than by the blood of Jesus, shed in profound love from a cross, inviting us to join his family.

Years ago, Judy Reilly, a writer from Baltimore, shared something that happened when she was standing in a shopping line with her three-year-old son, Joe. It was a long, long line, and over the minutes of their waiting, Joe was very curious about the people he saw and frequently asked, "Why does he or she do that or act like that?"

> "Suddenly (Reilly writes), Joe saw a person who left him speechless. A boy, a few years older than he, was being pushed into the store in a wheelchair. Joe took in every detail of the child—the boy's braced legs, slumped posture, tilted head, crooked smile, drool, and difficulty in speaking. As the boy got closer, I held my breath, hoping

that Joe would stay quiet, that he would stop staring, and that maybe we could even get out of the store. Just as the boy got within hearing distance, Joe looked at him and then glanced up at me, opened his mouth and smiled. 'Mommy,' he said, 'that boy has an Orioles cap just like mine!'" (Atlanta Constitution, 12-14-89).

Church is our spiritual family gathered around Jesus. The only way we can begin looking like it, and even more importantly *being* it, is to look past the differences, defects, limitations, failures, unpleasantness, and even the sins of one another, to see someone we recognize, someone we can relate to, someone that makes us feel right at home—Jesus, the gift we give each other.

> *Dear Lord, enter my heart and give me the vision to see you in my brothers and sisters in Christ. And then, please change me through what I see and receive. In Jesus' name, amen.*

JUNE 8

EQUALITY

Scripture for Reflection: 1 Corinthians 12:23-24

Yesterday, we saw how the key to Jesus' followers realizing the oneness for which Jesus prayed was for them to see him in each other. In John 17:21 Jesus described how this happens: the oneness relates to the way the Father is in the Son and the Son is in the Father (v. 21b). And further still: the Father and the Son also reside in his followers (v. 21c). In other words, the oneness of the Trinity is the pattern for relationships within the church. And here's the sobering thought: without that oneness in the church, the world will not believe that Jesus was sent by the Father (v. 21d). In other words, a church's credibility before the world lies with her oneness.

We know that the three Persons of the Trinity are 'co-equal in power and glory.' How can a congregation possibly match that? By the very nature of their positions in the church, some members wield more power and authority than others; and some, by their particular gifting, receive more public exposure and attention. I think we can begin to understand Jesus' meaning, however, when we understand not the worldly meaning of power and glory, but the spiritual. We all know what power looks like in the world in which we live. It is the power to control people and resources; it is power *over* something or someone. And in the world, glory is getting recognition, publicity, and prominence. The pursuit of both power and glory for oneself is no part of the kingdom of God and, therefore, can be no part of Christ. Sadly, it often infects the church.

No wonder there are turf wars, family squabbles, and underhanded moves in many churches. The pursuit of greater power and glory is clearly the cause. We so easily forget or fail to recognize the 'co-equal' part, the *shared* power and glory, the equality the Spirit gives. Instead, church becomes the venue for power plays and self-promotion. You may have come to the conclusion that since we all have our flaws, this behavior is normal and to be expected.

Yes, we all do have our flaws, and we have our moments when we say or do something to a brother or sister in Christ that honors the Christ in neither them nor us. We may have demeaned or devalued them. We may have even clothed our words or actions in garments of spiritual superiority. This can only happen when we are not seeing the Christ in them and not following the Christ in us. All is not lost, however. Having looked down on a brother or sister, we can confess our sin of treating them as less than equal to us, followed by asking forgiveness from God and from them. In doing so sincerely from the heart, we place them and ourselves within our love for Christ before whom we are equal and outside him empty.

We may object about the equality part. Yes, we obviously differ in our talents and capacities. Some are more suited for positions of leadership, so they have more public exposure. We see them at the front and center of things. They may seem to have more important roles. In thinking that is the case, we may well be mistaken. Power and prominence have nothing to do with

RENEWALS

spiritual depth. If we haven't observed humble souls exerting quiet, life-changing influence, we probably haven't been looking.

We know why Paul tells the Corinthian church to give the greater honor to those considered the lesser members of Christ's Body. Paul is attacking the spiritual arrogance of those who enjoy the power and attention of their position. He is inviting us to seek the Christ in *all* of us. Letting ourselves see Christ in those we may otherwise be tempted to consider "the least" of our fellow disciples will improve the accuracy of our spiritual insight. Christ is our true equalizer. Undervaluing any one of us is undervaluing him.

Dear Jesus, I want you to live in me. I ask that you give me the gift of humility, so that the Christ in me will see the Christ in all my fellow disciples, so the world will believe. Amen.

JUNE 9

FRIENDSHIP

Scripture for Reflection: John 15:9-17

In John 15, Jesus calls his disciples "friends," and he says it in a way that seems to supersede their place as servants. In that day servants followed orders and could not presume to know or understand the complete picture of their master's enterprise. Jesus seemed to be describing a deeper relationship between close friends for life. The claim of a personal friendship with God was unprecedented in the pagan world of that day. The gods kept their distance, interacting with humans only to make two-way deals. There is an interesting early reference in Jewish history to Moses's relationship with God during the forty years in the wilderness. Alone in the tent-tabernacle, he met with the Lord "face to face," *like friends* (Exodus 33:11a, italics added).

Paul sometimes used the word "reconcile" or "reconciliation" to describe what Jesus made possible for us through his life, death, and resurrection. The word is comprised of two Latin words: *re* (back) and *conciliare* (bring together). Reconciliation is literally 'bringing back together' what has been divided or torn asunder. In terms of our relationships, it is for us who were sinners, alienated from God, now becoming not only his human creation but his friends as well.

The friendship-with-God part is not as easy as it may seem.

RENEWALS

We can't just 'name it and claim it' and store it away for safe keeping. And we certainly can't play on God as our own Buddy, as some may try to do, reducing their relationship with him to a kind of private friendship cult without accountability for how we live our lives. Being a friend of God is a blessing we live out in three ways. First, we spend time with God, as we would with any close friend, sharing the things that are important to both of us. Second, we bring others into our conversation with God because our friendship with God includes them. And third, we ask him for the grace and wisdom to help pave a way for him to make enemies into friends—God's friends and our friends.

This brings us back to Jesus, the incarnate Son of God who, near the very end of his life, startled his disciples by calling them not just servants, or followers, or disciples—but *friends*. True friends love one another, help one another, give their lives for one another (John 15:13). They do what Jesus did for them as well as for us. This is our God, who *is* love, doing what love does. It's God in Jesus teaching us how to live in this kingdom of God he couldn't stop talking about, painting a huge portrait of how love lives, and assuring us there is a place in the picture for each one of us friends.

Does the prospect of being Jesus' kind of friend overwhelm you some? It does me. I'm a bit of a perfectionist; maybe you are, too. The fact is that God knows we won't be perfect at it in this life. But there can be moments when the power of Jesus' friendship breaks through in our relationships with one another. I remember John Hoggard, in a Bible conference message I heard years ago, referring to a verbal exchange between him and a friend over a situation in which each felt the other had wronged him. The heated exchange finally came to a standstill. In the relative calm that ensued, Hoggard said, "Dear friend, the Christ in me is not going to argue with the Christ in you." And they were friends again.

Our friendship with God and with others is God's gift. When we answer to his gift of friendship, he calls us to befriend others. We typically gravitate toward some more than others because they are more appealing to us, or more like us. And Christ says, "Yes, do have friends you're more comfortable with. But don't fail also to befriend those who are unappealing, because if you take the risk of seeing and trusting me in them, they will teach what your more natural friends can't, and you will much more fully know what friendship with me is."

Dear loving Father, thank you for the grace of your friendship. Dear Jesus, saving friend, show me how to be a true friend of God and of the persons who come my way. Dear Holy Spirit, empower me to live the life of friendship to which Jesus calls me. I pray this in his name, who befriended me and made me his friend and a friend of others. Amen.

JUNE 10

Forgiveness

Scripture for Reflection: Ephesians 4:32; Colossians 3:12-15; Matthew 5:43-49

God is a forgiver. We can't earn his forgiveness, no more than we can earn his love. As his love comes to us undeserved, so does his forgiveness. Love and forgiveness are his nature, and we receive them humbly on our knees.

How do we know we've really been forgiven by God? We know by the effect God's forgiveness has on us. If it changes us so that we set off to become forgivers ourselves, God is pleased. Even though we don't do it perfectly, we get better at it. Sometimes we forget that forgiveness is never earned; it is always a gift when it is given. Forgiveness doesn't say, "If you do this or that, I'll forgive you. And if you don't, I won't." Forgiveness doesn't come with conditions.

On the other hand, Jesus clearly teaches that God's forgiveness is meant to change us, not let us off the hook. To put it more positively, *God forgives us in order to make forgivers of us* (Matthew 6:12, 14). God, of course, doesn't need forgiveness. The acts of forgiveness he calls us to are directed toward others, anyone who needs it, whether or not they ask for it, whether or not they own up to what they have done.

Sometimes *we* are the ones standing in the need of forgiveness.

Sometimes we need to apologize and ask for forgiveness. This may be difficult if we have a high opinion of ourselves, or see ourselves as always kind and loving, or are perfectionists who can't face our imperfections. Or, for others, asking for forgiveness is too easy, either because of low self-esteem or a superficial desire to get it all over with and not really understand the hurt and damage done. For all of us, sincerely apologizing and asking for forgiveness takes courage. Asking for forgiveness is exposing our vulnerability. We run the risk of our apology not being accepted and forgiveness not granted.

Who are those that Christ calls us to forgive? First, they are the ones we're closest to—family, friends, and others we are associated with. Here, the pain is probably deeper because we were confident of their love and respect for us, so their hurtful act seems almost a betrayal. Second, Christ calls us to forgive people we come across in our daily lives but are not close to. It may be easier to forgive them when they say or do something that sounds demeaning to us, since little has been invested in the relationship. And third, Christ calls us to forgive our enemies—those who do not like us and seem committed to undermine, denigrate, or even destroy us in some way. Forgiving those we love and are closest to draws on the strength and commitment of the relationship. Forgiving those we're not close to is probably easier because the investment in the relationship is smaller. Forgiving someone who despises our very existence and in one way or another is trying to disempower or even obliterate us is the most difficult forgiveness. Such forgiveness is the irrefutable proof of God's love shaping our heart and changing our mind. In this divided, hating world, the power of this forgiveness is transformative.

RENEWALS

Receiving forgiveness begins with apologizing and confessing. Real friends apologize and ask forgiveness, and real friends accept apologies and forgive. Asking forgiveness and giving forgiveness can be hard to do. But we have the whole Trinity behind us. We have the Father who is love (1 John 4:7), which is where forgiveness originates; we have the Son, who on the Cross pleaded forgiveness for the crucifiers, who represent the whole lot of us (Luke 23:34); and we have the resurrected Jesus breathing the Holy Spirit on that pathetic band of defeated disciples and gifting them with the power of forgiveness (John 20:22-23). We are friends of God and one another, and godly friends forgive as they have been forgiven.

Loving Father, thank you for forgiving me of my sins, for giving me Jesus who taught me how to be a forgiver, and for releasing your Holy Spirit into the world to empower me with forgiving love. I ask you to sanctify me to make enemies into friends through Jesus. Amen.

JUNE 11

Fellowship

Scripture for Reflection: John 20:19-23

The word "religion" comes from the Latin word *religare*, which means 'to bind together.' Think of all the things Christians have in common, the things that bind them together. We could break it down into a multitude of doctrines and practices. Ah, but there are disagreements over some doctrines, and another church's practices—style of worship, for example—may make members of our particular church very uneasy. So, what is it that binds *all* Christians together? It is *Christ himself*, the full expression of the Father's love and the central focus of the Holy Spirit's influence. The church is *his* Body, and each of us is a part of that Body (1 Corinthians 12:27a), or we are not a part of him.

That kind of claim is heresy in a world that promotes and rewards our individual pursuits, our drive for financial success, our publicized achievements—and in the process, gives credit to no one but ourselves. We even have some carefully packaged Christian superstars with their own take on the gospel, building private empires that seduce thousands with their facile take on Jesus. Listen carefully to what the superstar says and does. Is he prospering by getting his followers to live by his own teaching, or is he leading them to live in the kingdom of God that Jesus taught? Is he inviting people to build a self-made Christian kingdom of success, or is he inviting them to seek God's kingdom as a part of the Body of Christ?

An American missionary serving in Africa tells about leaving for his homeland furlough in the States. As he prepared to board the plane, an African lady in the church group seeing him off hugged him and said, "When you get back to your home church, please be sure to say hello to the rest of us." *The rest of us*. That lady understood that we don't stand alone as followers of Jesus. We stand together across the world. As different as we may look, as far away as we may live, as varied as our practices and styles of worship are, we stand together as a part of God's one household (Ephesians 2:19), brothers and sisters in Christ (Matthew 23:8b), even across every boundary—physical, national, racial, and ethnic (John 11:52).

The 'binding together' of the church in Christ is God's gift. Sometimes it's messy, even within the same congregation. As church pastor Martha Tatarnic puts it,

> True liberation is found in letting go of that relentless search for individual salvation and allowing yourself to be stuck with a salvation that must be negotiated in community. Allowing yourself to be stuck also means your salvation isn't riding on one fragile little life figuring it out alone, but rather on your participation in a hope that God is already enacting. It means that you can expect not only that your little life will bear blessings for others, but also that others—even as sometimes you would rather close the gate on them—are going to bless you too ("Freedom from Family?", CC, 2/26/20, p. 11).

The current 'cult of self' is an insidious threat to authentic

Christian faith and practice. Christ calls us to live in community with God and in community with each other. How we live out that identity in our congregation and in the world near and far is a matter of discernment and conscience. "Conscience" is an interesting word. It is comprised of two words that mean "knowing" and "together." By the very definition of the word, our consciences are formed and corrected in a community. In the community of Jesus' followers, we develop a godly conscience. Without Christian fellowship centered on Christ and grounded in Scripture, we will lose our way in a world all too prepared to lure us to a life that corrupts our soul and demeans our character.

As you think about the church that holds your membership, reflect also on your own identification with that community and your participation in its life and mission. Is there something of yourself Christ is asking you to offer? And is there something you need personally for your journey with Christ that this community of faith can be helpful with?

> *Dear Lord, save me from the illusion that I can be your disciple without your Body, the church. Help me to be a better member of my church by receiving the teaching, participating in the process of discerning your will, and offering myself and the gifts I have to serving my fellow members. I ask these things in your name. Amen.*

JUNE 12

HUMILITY

Scripture for Reflection: Matthew 18:1-5; 23:12

Dr. Joseph Parker, a well-known and respected congregational preacher in nineteenth-century England, had a conversation with a highly successful business magnate. During their exchange, the businessman said to Parker, "I'm a self-made man, you know." To which Parker, tongue-in-cheek, replied, "Sir, you have lifted a great load of responsibility from the Almighty."

The cult of the self-built life continues to this day. Countless seminars are available to advise us and give us tools to become a self-made success in just about any field we want to pursue in order to make a name for ourselves and to garner praise and admiration. This happens not only outside the church; it happens inside as well. We expect it outside the church, but when this approach motivates us inside the Body of Christ, we have lost our moorings.

Of course, we would like for our church to grow and succeed. Jesus' life, death, and resurrection launched a movement that flooded the Mediterranean world with his gospel, and the church grew rapidly—but *humbly*. They were not looking to a Jesus who was a worldly success; they were looking to a Jesus who preferred the company of those of lower status, a Jesus who made the high-profile people uncomfortable, the Jesus who emptied himself. They followed the lowly Jesus, the Jesus who preferred to be with the people considered losers. They followed the Jesus who washed feet, who didn't hold his disciples' blunders against them, who followed the strategies of his heart rather that the calculations of his mind. They followed the real Jesus, not a political Jesus, not a success-driven Jesus.

How, then, did this young church manage to grow like wildfire? They were certainly not perfect. Prejudice between Jewish and pagan converts had to be resolved again and again. Discrimination against the poor members by wealthier members had to be confronted. Promiscuous behaviors that had characterized the previous lives of some of the pagan converts had to be discontinued. These issues were addressed not so much by the rigid enforcement of rules as by the example of Jesus' life.

Jesus had some words for those who were wearing themselves out in their striving and were overburdened with the heavy loads of their pursuits: "Put on *my* yoke, and learn from *me*. I'm gentle and humble. And you will find rest for yourselves. My yoke is easy to bear, and my burden is light" (Matthew 11:29-30, italics added). Don't take the 'easy yoke' part wrongly. The easy yoke is the life we were created and redeemed for. It is the yoke that fits a follower of Jesus, and when the life we are living fits who we really are, there is a naturalness about it. Jesus' words are not words for an easy road, however. Humility is not particularly popular. In a world of blatant self-advancement, living a life of humility requires courage. People who are driven by the lust to succeed will probably, in one way or another, ignore, oppose, alienate, or isolate the humble of spirit. True humility is a silent rebuke of those who see it as a judgment on their desperate pursuit of the gods of power that they serve.

RENEWALS

How, then, can we cultivate this Christlike humility? The church is its breeding ground. Peter is speaking to all the churches scattered across five Roman provinces when he writes, "And everyone, clothe yourselves with humility toward each other. God stands against the proud, but he gives favor to the humble" (1 Peter 5:5b). Are we ready to let Jesus lower us to his level? Are we ready to be humbled so that we can discover and find our true selves?

Dear Lord, help me to humble myself before my brothers and sisters in Christ, so that I can be ready to travel the path of humility in this world where you call me to act like you and love others as you do. I pray in your name. Amen.

June 13
Together in Service
Scripture for Reflection: Luke 22:24-27

Humility is the gift through which our service is service as Jesus taught, lived, and called us to practice it. He was known to describe himself as someone who was among them to serve, not to wield authority like a king, not to lord it over others, but to be, if you like, the servant at their table. Which, by the way, is the literal meaning of the Greek word in the passage: 'table server.' It's the word from which Christianity gets the word "deacon." It was first used in Acts to designate a special order within the church to serve food to the Greek-speaking widows who were being ignored. Lest we see these deacons as capable only of serving tables, Acts tells us that those chosen were "well respected and endowed by the Spirit with exceptional wisdom" (Acts 6:1-3). One of them was Stephen, the first Christian martyr who, before his death by stoning, gave eloquent testimony to Jesus as the fulfillment of the Jewish hope (Acts 6:8; 7:60).

Jesus used the term not in the literal sense of 'table server' but as a way to profile a disciple's heart motivated by Christlike love. It begins with Jesus' command for his disciples to wash one another's feet. Not to be missed in the picture is the background of a meal or a banquet where the feet of guests were washed by house servants or by the host himself when there were no servants. Jesus was again identifying humble service as the calling of *every disciple*, no exceptions. He concluded the subject by suggesting that his disciples would be truly happy only if their fellowship together had this character of serving one another (John 13:14-17).

Much of what we have said about the church in previous meditations is expressed here. Inclusiveness (serving people not like us); sharing our journeys; oneness, equality, friendship within the Body of Christ; acts of mutual forgiveness, fellowship, and humility—all these come together in shaping the character of our service to one another. Most of all, this servant calling is modeled after Jesus. "I am among you as one who serves," he said to his disciples when he overheard them arguing about which one of them was the greatest in his circle. Greatness, said Jesus, was not measured by the power one wielded but by the lower status one claimed. True leadership was measured by the depth of a person's genuine servanthood (Luke 22:24-27).

Servanthood begins with those we're closest to—family, those we fellowship and worship with. But it doesn't stop there, as it didn't with Jesus. He told us to bring fellow Christians who were far away into the orbit of our servanthood. A beautiful example of this was discovered by the apostle Paul in the churches of Macedonia, who sacrificially gave of their resources to serve famine-stricken Christians in Judea:

> *"They were being tested by many problems, their extra amount of happiness and their extreme poverty resulted in a surplus of rich generosity ... they gave what they could afford, and even more than they could afford, and they did it voluntarily. They urgently begged us for the privilege of sharing in this service for the saints. They even exceeded our*

expectations, because they gave themselves to the Lord first and to us, consistent with God's will" (2 Corinthians 8:2-5).

The scope of our servanthood does not even stop here. Jesus also asks us to serve those considered 'the least': the hungry and thirsty, the strangers, the poorly clothed, the sick, the imprisoned—whatever their spiritual state or their religion may be (Matthew 25:31-46). And then the toughest of all his expectations: love our enemies. I'm certain he doesn't mean to love them abstractly in our minds or silently in our hearts. God's love is neither abstract nor hidden; nor can ours be. God doesn't love without acting on it. The nature of divine love is to express, not withhold it. The nature of God's love in us is to humble ourselves, even before enemies, and serve them. Can you imagine the difference that would make in this divided world?

Dear Lord, please grant me the status of your lowliness, the gift of your inclusive love, and the grace to serve those I find to be the most difficult. I ask in the name of Jesus. Amen.

June 14

Together in Suffering

Scripture for Reflection: Romans 5:8-11; Galatians 2:20

Recently I came across a painting on a book cover that intrigued me. The title of the book is *The Love that Is God: An Invitation to Christian Faith*, by Frederick C. Bauerschmidt. What caught my immediate attention was the section of a painting of the Crucifixion used on the upper part of the cover. It was by Laurent Girardin. I researched the painting and found that it now resides in the Cleveland Museum of Art, where I was able to see the entire painting online. It is oil on wood dated 1460. What drew me to the painting was the depiction of the Trinity—Father, Son, and Holy Spirit, *together in suffering*.

In the foreground and at the center of the painting is Jesus on the cross. God the Father is close behind him, seeming to be looking directly at us. His arms are stretched to both sides, and his hands are grasping the crossbeam of the cross. He is a participant in his Son's suffering. Just above Jesus' haloed head sits a symbol of the Holy Spirit, a beautiful white dove, stretching out its wings to call attention to what is happening, silent in the face of a deep pain.

One of the ways we misrepresent the Trinity is to treat the Persons like separate people, each with their own feelings and experiences. For example, we may speak of God the Father sending his Son to earth, incarnate in Jesus, to suffer and be crucified for our sins, while he remains a safe, heavenly distance away. Some have objected that, from this perspective, God comes across as a spectator while his Son goes through horror. They may even say that God the Father becomes a divine child abuser. Furthermore, the action that wins our salvation is reduced to a transaction that corresponds to the pagan sacrifices we discussed in the June 1 meditation. Some of the pagan religions in biblical times practiced human sacrifice. You will remember the story of God telling Abraham to sacrifice his son Isaac to test Abraham's faith, and then at the last minute staying his hand, thereby declaring the end of this despicable transactional practice.

We often say, or have heard it said, that Jesus was sent to die for our sins, and that it was not enough that he simply die; he had to die the most painful death in order to 'purchase' our salvation. The price he paid for our salvation was enormous enough to cancel the debt of all our sins. It trades on the truth that Jesus was the only person of sufficient spiritual perfection to make the sacrifice sufficient. It is still, however, transactional, and as such, it leads so many to conclude that since Jesus *paid* it all, well, there's not much I need to do. "Thank you, Lord!"

But wait. What about those passages calling us to *our own* crucifixion? Paul talks about "our old self" having been "crucified with him so that the body of sin might be done away with, that we should no longer be slaves to sin…" (Romans 6:6). Or his personal testimony in Galatians 2:20: "I have been crucified with Christ and I no longer live, but Christ lives in me…" In other words, the Crucifixion of the Son of God wasn't an event that gets us off the hook; it was an event that draws us in. In a world of rampant sin, the inevitable outcome of living the life of Jesus is some form of suffering. The gift of his sacrifice is the power to live his life even in these circumstances.

This is a distinct departure from seeing Jesus' death as transactional. It isn't. Jesus' death is *transformational*. It is transformational because of the life he taught and lived. And it is transformational because the Father's loving presence and the Holy Spirit's power were with him all the way to and through the Cross. We followers of Jesus may not suffer the horrible physical abuse Jesus did, but we all will suffer the rejection and abuse of a world of people who are set on worshiping only themselves and on living in the lies they create to justify their self-absorption.

Dear Jesus, I join you, with the Father and the Spirit, in feeling the pain of your crucifixion for loving the world. I seek your love, which is beyond my meager understanding and powerful beyond my earthly loves. Take away my obsessions with my own interests, I ask in your world-loving, life-giving name. Amen.

WEEKS 3–5
RELATIONAL COVENANTS

"Covenant" is an interesting word. When we covenant, we're usually promising that we will indeed do what we pledge to do about something. When we enter *into* a covenant with someone or some group, we and they either give our word to honor what we've agreed to, or we sign a document outlining exactly what the obligations of all parties to the contract are. Increasingly, covenants are legal documents to ensure that each party does what they pledge to do, or else suffer a prescribed penalty. The increased legalization of covenants may well be a measure of the breakdown of our capacity to trust one another.

Students of Scripture will know that God is a covenant-making God. The earliest use of the Hebrew word "covenant" (*berith*) in the Old Testament occurs in God's dealings with Noah, just before the Great Flood (Genesis 6:17-18); he promises to make a covenant with Noah following the flood. Once the ark is on dry land again, and because of Noah's obedience, God makes a covenant with him never again to cut off life by floodwaters (9:8-11). It is interesting that the covenant includes "all the animals of the earth." The sign of this extensive covenant would be the rainbow.

From that point on, God's covenant with his chosen people develops further and shapes the narrative of his relationship with them. He promises their wellbeing and prosperity if they obey his instructions. When they don't, they suffer the consequences. As we move into the era of the prophets, however, the covenant takes on a deeper, more personal character. God becomes the divine Lover who pours out his heart for his people, pleased when they prove their love for him, hurt when they ignore him and take him for granted. In the interpretation of the prophet Hosea, God's chosen people are his beloveds who have abandoned him for false lovers; and like a true Lover, he will charm them back (Hosea 2:14-15), establish a new covenant with them, and restore their fortunes (2:16-20). The covenant, which by that time has become largely defined by obedience to the Law, is now defined as "faithful love" between God and his people and a relationship between two parties who really want to know each other on a deeper level (6:6). The covenant has become relational, with love at the center of it.

Transition to the New Testament, and we see the coming of the Christ proclaimed as the fulfillment of this covenant (Luke 1:72), a covenant that through the life and death of Jesus now includes the Gentiles—i.e., the whole human race (Galatians 3:13-14). The sacrificial death of Jesus, "the one offering for all time," eliminates any further need for a sacrifice for sins. The writer to the Hebrews goes on to quote from Jeremiah 31:33: "I will place my laws in their hearts/ and write them on their minds" (Hebrews 10:14-17). Jesus himself becomes "the mediator of the new covenant" through the blood proof of his sacrifice (12:24).

This is the new covenant that fulfills the deepest intention of the old covenant (Matthew 5:17). It is love-based because *love is who and what God IS* (1 John 4:16). Love is also what God *DOES* (John 3:16). Love—his kind of love—is what he gives and releases in us (1 John 4:7). And the person who has no relationship with God cannot love God's way (v.8).

Over the next three weeks we will explore the three dimensions of this love covenant with God through Christ. It is a covenant in which God's love is lived out in three settings:

- In our personal relationship with God (Week 3: Personal Covenants, June 15–21).
- In our relationships in the Body of Christ (Week 4: Church Covenants, June 22–28).
- In our relationships in and with the world (Week 5: World Covenants, June 29–July 5).

OUR PERSONAL COVENANTS

JUNE 15

A Covenant of Intimacy

Scripture for Reflection: John 8:43-47a; 15:15; James 1:5

The renowned fifteenth-century painter and monk Fra Angelico once said, "He [or she] who wishes to paint Christ's story must live with Christ." Painting Christ's story is a vivid way of describing our calling as his disciples to capture enough of his nature to help an observer visualize him. The key to it, says Fra Angelico, is to "live with Christ." For so many Christians, that is the challenge unmet, or to say it better, the privilege not taken, or even better, the intimacy not engaged.

Through Christ, God wants to live with us. He is our Divine Lover. True lovers spend time together because they make time. Since God is always available, the decision to make time lies with us. We can diligently set aside time—say, first thing in the morning—for our devotions. This is a good first step. But what really happens during that devotional time?

We might decide to begin with reading and meditating on a Scripture passage as part of a study of a book in the Bible. We might consult other translations, maybe even a Bible commentary, for better understanding. We might turn parts of the reading into a personal prayer. We might also read a book of devotions or some other helpful book by a Christian author. We might then spend time in prayers of praise, adoration, confession, or intercession.

We may do all this and still not enter into intimacy with God. We may be enlightened in our minds and perhaps even moved emotionally, but we're not closer to God, not more in touch with his heart, not allowing his love to penetrate our heart. I do not say this to disparage devotions that are implemented consistently. On the contrary, those who seek to follow Jesus on the run, or who, when pressed for time, eliminate their devotional time as the first alternative, are living under the illusion that their spirituality will not suffer for lack of cultivation. No intimate relationship and certainly no spiritual covenant can survive by being taken for granted. Think of a marriage where there is little to no communication at a deeper level. It will either not survive, or if it does, it will be only a cooperative partnership, or at worst a pretense.

I must confess that it took me some time to discover that prayer really *is* two-way communication and that the *key* communicator is God through Christ. Before then, I approached prayer as me bringing my concerns to God and asking him to fix or solve them—and I usually didn't fail to define or at least suggest what these fixes or solutions were. In other words, I saw God as a power source for implementing my own wishes. Now, these wishes of mine weren't necessarily unworthy; some of them were quite decent, I thought. But they were petitions delivered with ready-made solutions. I was trying to manipulate God, who can't be manipulated.

Matthew records the voice of God on the Mount of Jesus' Transfiguration: "This is my Son whom I dearly love ... *Listen to him!*" (Matthew 17:5b, italics added). What was missing in my prayers was the listening. God had plenty he wanted me to know, but my ears were closed. In my devotions I finally began to focus on listening. I now start my time of meditation by listening to God say to me, "Be still and know that I am God" (Psalm 46:10a, NRSV). And I still myself to hear him. This is where Scripture is so important. I test what I hear by what the Bible has to say about God, and especially by the kind of life Jesus calls us to live and the way he calls us to love in Scripture.

I'm growing in my relationship with God as it becomes more and more a covenant of shared, two-way intimacy. How about you?

> *Thank you, Lord, for caring for me and listening to me.*
> *Help me to incline my ears to you so as not to miss your*
> *voice, your words, your love, your will, and your wisdom.*
> *And having heard, help me by your grace to paint a better*
> *picture of Christ today. I ask in his name. Amen.*

JUNE 16

A Covenant of Transparency

Scripture for Reflection: 1 John 1:5-10

We are called to be transparent because God is transparent. He hides nothing about himself from us: his nature, his love, his displeasure, his heartbreak, his joy, his grace, and a thousand other things that are revealed in Scripture or in our own life experiences. He takes on no form or appearance that is not who he is. Created in his image, we are called to reflect that transparency, to reveal who and what we really are. And there's the rub. It may not be a pretty picture.

Does God expect us to reveal our sins and faults to the world, like exhibitionists or masochists? No, but he *would* like a posture of humility. "God," says Peter, "stands against the proud, but he gives grace to the humble" (1 Peter 5:5b, NRSV). Our humility is the sign that we are living in grace on our journey of becoming the humans God created us to be, though we haven't yet arrived. We admit our imperfections, not as permanent brandings, but as marks of where God is still at work to perfect us.

The way forward on that journey of perfecting is called *confession*. Confession of our imperfections and sins requires *transparency*. We cannot see what we need to confess unless we remove the obstructions, cover-ups, and deceptions that enable us to hide the sin. These false fronts give us false protections.

They make us look better or more innocent than we are. They project a lie. Confession, on the other hand, begins with the search for truth about ourselves and focuses on the unpleasant truths, in the assurance that the confession of them will bring God's forgiveness and the Spirit's power to overcome them (1 John 1:9). Therese of Lisieux, a nineteenth-century Carmelite nun, spoke of such courageous confessions in these words: "If you are willing to bear the trial of being displeasing to yourself, then you will be for Jesus a pleasant place of shelter." Our confessions are not embarrassments to our Lord; they draw his love and forgiveness, and they open up more space for him to dwell in us.

Confessions also often draw others into our lives. What we need to confess may require the help of another trustworthy person or spiritual counselor with whom we are willing to be transparent. Or we may need to confess to someone with whom we were deceptive or not transparent. This takes courage; the courage that comes with true humility, which is given to those who sincerely ask.

There is another important way to practice transparency. We may unknowingly stand in someone's way and make it more difficult for the light of God to get through to him or her. The obstructive shadow we cast could be our dominance, our overpowering influence, our stubbornness, our biases, or our strong viewpoints. We may, in love, need to step aside and allow God's light to illumine the heart and mind of the one on whom we are, perhaps unknowingly, casting a shadow of control. We may need to let go and back off so that the person can see for him or herself. This may be how we best give someone the gift of clear sight.

Our transparency makes it possible for us to see and confess our own sin. It also allows the rays of God's light not only to

RENEWALS

convey but also to amplify the light to others. Either way, transparency is God's gift to us all.

Is there a next step for you to take toward an honest, accurate look at yourself? Or perhaps toward being a better facilitator of God's light to someone else?

> *Christ Jesus, Light of the World, please give me the gift of a transparent life, so that I can see myself truthfully and confess those spiritual imperfections that obscure your image in me. Sanctify my heart and guide my living so that I will be a channel of your light and your love to others. I ask this in your name and for your glory. Amen.*

JUNE 17

A Covenant of Grace

Scripture for Reflection: Luke 18:9-14; 1 Corinthians 15:9-10

In our day, a covenant requires a commitment from all parties in order to be effective. Our covenant with God, however, is different. It is a covenant of grace. Applying the word "grace" to our covenant with God says that he is the originator of this covenant and the sole source of its benefit. One party (God) is the giver, and the others (us) are the receivers.

Do you mean that the receiving party can do nothing to merit or earn their place in the covenant? That we, all of us, are undeserving of God's salvation in Christ and the benefits that accrue from our covenant membership with him? Yes, that is indeed true. In fact, that un-deservedness is at the heart of every true act of grace. When the apostle Paul says, "I am what I am by God's grace," in 1 Corinthians 15:10, he is saying he brought nothing to his salvation save his open arms and receiving heart. Grace is always a gift, and every true gift is an act of grace. It gives Paul more than he deserves, while astonishingly testifying to his infinite worth.

Jesus tells the story of two people praying in church. One of them seems very grateful to God for how his life has turned out. He goes on to enumerate the blessings in very specific ways by comparing himself to lesser souls who are clearly not as spiritually fortunate, and probably not as deserving as he. The other man, however, stands back at a distance, hunched over and refusing even to look up toward heaven. He seems uncomfortable, ill at ease, out of place. Well, he *is* out of place in this church that honors the spiritual achievers, the religious superstars, the models of holiness. He strikes his chest, not as a boastful gesture, but to accentuate and own his sinfulness. As he does so, he shouts out in grieving despair, "God, show mercy to me, a sinner!"

We can imagine how disturbing his bold interruption of the course of worship is in church that day—a church that honors religious achievement, strength not weakness, naming and claiming the blessing, and definitely *not* personal honesty about one's sinfulness. The transparency and humility of the tax collector is embarrassing. How can he live with himself, and presume to invade the sacred precincts with his unworthiness?

How can he presume? Jesus shocks us by claiming that this tax collector, rather than the superstar, is the one who goes back to his home justified. This outcome turns religion on its head. Jesus says we are justified by confessing our unworthiness, not by bragging about our righteousness. We enter into a covenant with God not by what we bring to the table, but by what we confess we can't bring. Our place at the table is given to us by grace.

This all may sound as if Jesus is denigrating righteous living and glorifying sinfulness. Nothing could be further from the truth. What he is doing is exposing the sin of self-righteousness and pride in our "spiritual accomplishments." In fact, Jesus saves his harshest criticism for this group. The confessing sinner in the parable is fully aware of his sin and of his own inability to overcome it. In his helplessness he knows his only hope is undeserved grace. The spiritual superstar has much further to go because he is blind to the way the sin of his own self-righteousness has taken the place of a true, love-based holiness.

Sometimes we forget that the saving covenant with God through Christ that we have entered is *always* a covenant of undeserved grace. Indeed, God's grace enables us to grow in likeness to Christ, but that likeness itself is a gift. It is nothing to be proud of, only grateful for. As the hymn says, "'Tis grace has brought me safe thus far/ and grace will lead me home."

God of grace, if I am like that sinful tax collector, help me to trust your grace to free me to become and live as a disciple of Jesus. Or, if I am more like the self-righteous pharisee, humble me to confess my spiritual arrogance and my utter need of your grace, to the very end of my journey on earth. I pray this in the name of Jesus, your grace in human flesh. Amen.

JUNE 18

A COVENANT OF ATTENTIVENESS

Scripture for Reflection: Luke 19:1-10; 16:19-31

In Harriet Doerr's novel, *Stones for Ibarra*, Richard and Sara Everton, a middle-aged married couple, drive from their home in California to Ibarra, Mexico where Richard's father abandoned his copper mine during the Revolution of 1910. Sara is not sure why they are doing this and what her husband hopes to find. Richard does eventually succeed in reopening the mine and extracting copper. But this is not the treasure. The treasure proves to be the people and the places they inhabit, the culture and the characters, the exposed, unadorned humanness.

Four months after Richard's death, Sara is sitting by the window during a rain, thinking of the people in the region of Ibarra she and Richard had come to know and the roads they lived on. Here's the thought that settles in her mind: "... Nothing ever happened on either numbered or unnumbered roads that could be classified as unimportant. All of it, observed by dark, observed by day, was extraordinary" (Penguin Books, 1985, p. 207).

I think that seeing the world in this way is what Scripture is also inviting us to do. There are no insignificant places and no insignificant people inhabiting those places. Every person and every place *are* extraordinary if we pay close attention. Wherever

Jesus was and whoever was there drew his attention. And just to emphasize the point, he very intentionally spent most of his time with those who were considered ordinary or unimportant. He did spend some time with high-profile people, but they either had to invite him over or crash his teaching party.

The covenant of grace into which Jesus calls us frees us to be attentive to where we are and who we're with. Let's be clear about the focus of that attentiveness. It is not the attentiveness exploited by the information economy. Along with the good that does come with Facebook—for example, the immediacy of connecting with friends and lending support—the platform incessantly bombards us with invitations to 'friend' more and more people. What the growing list leads to is the comfort of having a very large number of "friends" whom we don't actually *befriend*. Mostly they become our audience, and we theirs. We can become so absorbed in expanding our *list* of friends that we reduce our capacity to *be* friends in person. Just take a look at small gatherings of people and note how often conversation is interrupted by calls or posts.

Some studies have found that most people do not feel listened to. When author Kate Murphy asked people, "Who really listens to you?", most came up with one or two persons—usually a spouse, parent, best friend, or sibling. "Most admitted they didn't have anyone who truly listened to them. A few said they talk to a pastor or a rabbi, but only in a time of crisis. Most of the people who listen are paid to do it—therapists, life coaches, hairdressers, and astrologers" (Literary hub, 1-7-20). Are we becoming a world of non-listeners who in turn are not listened to?

The Internet is luring us to know people without really knowing them, to be someplace without really being there. In the

RENEWALS

process, we're becoming increasingly disconnected from the place where we are and the people around us. Add to this the effect of our culture of driven-ness to succeed, make a name, or earn a lot of money, all the while seeing others either as irrelevant to our goals or as potential competitors.

In this culture of inattentiveness, Jesus calls us to be attentive to the small place where we are and the ordinary people who populate it—until it all begins to look quite extraordinary, just as Jesus sees them.

Prayer suggestion: Think of the people around you, especially those who see themselves or are seen by others as the least significant. Be attentive to them in a way you think Jesus would, looking for and finding the extraordinary in them. Include them in your daily prayers.

June 19

A Covenant of Obedience

Scripture for Reflection: 2 Corinthians 10:1-5; 1 Peter 1:13-16

The covenant we have entered into with God calls us to obedience; specifically, obedience to Christ and to his way of life. Admittedly, obedience is a conflicted word these days. For example, some decide that a certain government law violates their individual rights. Others decide that another law promotes arbitrary discrimination. And they both choose to disobey those laws. In this world where obedience to just about anything can be challenged, what does our obedience to Christ mean? The answer is that, for the Christian, obedience is embracing not an idea but a Person who embodies what all of us were created for: loving God and others.

Christ is, in fact, our model of this obedience (Philippians 2:5). For us and our salvation, he "humbled himself by becoming obedient to the point of death, even death on a cross" (v. 8). Through his obedience, "many people were made righteous" (Romans 5:19). What that obedience intended for us is that we "be holy in every aspect of [our] lives," holy like *Jesus* (1 Peter 1:14b-15). In fact, God gives his sanctifying Holy Spirit only to those who obey him (Acts 5:32b). Christ's obedience was to God, and the laws he taught and obeyed were revealed in his teachings about the kingdom of God. His kingdom obedience was nothing less than our salvation (Romans 5:19), and its radical love-centeredness is our model.

How shall we describe this obedience? It is not obedience to a set of rules, but it will include abiding by certain guidelines Jesus outlined. It is not uncritical obedience to church leaders, but Christians do need the insights and guidance of good spiritual leaders. Then what exactly is this obedience? It is the obedience of love, or the obedience that love gives us and draws from us, the love to which God again and again beckons us in Scripture. As we have already seen, God *is* love, and the life and death of Jesus are the saving and sanctifying manifestations of that love. When the voice of God calls out to us from the mountain of Jesus' Transfiguration, we hear the commanding words, "Listen to him!" Listen to what you hear revealed in his life and in his words; allow what you see to speak to you, to teach you, to overwhelm you, to overtake your heart and guide your actions. Like Jesus, let your obedience be the vehicle of God's love.

The covenant relationship into which Jesus calls us binds us to live this love and embody it in our own lives. How is this done? How do we obey God's kind of love? We know this is our calling, but how do we let go of our self-centeredness, our unpleasantness, our impatience with others, our others-ignoring driven-ness—all the areas where we are unlike Christ? The answer may have a number of facets, but the foundation of them all is prayer. Not prayer first of all for what we think we need, but prayer for what God knows we need.

We become used to praying our petitions as if we know exactly what we or others need. It's prescribing what God needs to do. This is not coming boldly to the throne of grace; it is coming brazenly. It is us setting both the agenda and the proper outcome.

God has no problem with our sharing with him an outcome we would like or deeply want to see happen, so long as we agree he may well have a better plan, which may be more difficult or even painful for us.

Obedience in our covenant relationship with God means praying with listening ears, opening our hearts to his love so that our minds can see a more excellent way, which may not be the way we want. It may be love's tougher but triumphant way.

> *Thank you, Jesus, for obeying love, from birth to cross, from life to death—to resurrection. Forgive me for sometimes (or often) praying for what I want without taking the trouble to listen. Help me to discern how your love is at work in my life and in your world. By your Spirit, please empower me to obey love. I pray in your name. Amen.*

JUNE 20

A Covenant of New Revelations

Scripture for Reflection: Luke 10:23-24; 12:1-3; 1 Corinthians 2:6-16

"The secret things belong to the Lord our God. The revealed things belong to us and to our children forever: to keep all the words of this covenant." (Deuteronomy 29:29)

The writer of those words seems to be making an intentional distinction between what the Lord reveals to his people and what he doesn't. Consider "the revealed things." God does not want to keep us wondering about what he asks of us. He has made that much clear in Scripture. "Your word is a lamp before my feet and a light for the journey," says the psalmist (Psalm 119:105). The imagery is of someone on a journey who needs the provision of God's light in order to see and travel the way. The light (revelation) may come directly from Scripture or be mediated through the help of a friend or spiritual director, or it may come directly to the person as a word from an unseen source, like a divinely inspired epiphany.

Jesus was known for showering people with revelations that came as shocking epiphanies. On a number of occasions, he opened what he had to say with the phrase, "You have heard that it was said to those who lived long ago that … But I say to you…" What he was talking about was usually one of the covenant commandments that forbade a certain sin. He took that sin and internalized it, locating it in the intention of the person's heart, the source of the sin. So, for example, the prohibition of murder now becomes the prohibition and confession of the anger and hatred one has toward another—a murder, if you like, in the heart, though not carried out in person (Matthew 5:21-22a). Just when we think we're obeying one of God's commandments, we're told that our obedience could be pretense. "Proper" religious behavior may hide a deeper disobedience. This may well explain Jesus' frequent hostility toward those who took pride in their model behavior based on strict observance of the Torah. He knew their behavior did not reflect their hearts.

God sees the hidden. He sees the beauty of the love that resides in our heart, even though our expression of it might be awkward and clumsy. He also sees the ugliness of our self-centered heart, even though our conduct may be a pretending to care. Our covenant with God through Christ is forged within the mystery of an unquantifiable love. When we allow that love to start taking over our hearts, we begin to become channels of grace. This grace frees us to love as Christ does. It travels from the purified heart of God to the purifying of our own hearts to giving us the grace-given ability to love others. None of this can be calculated or conjured; it can only be received with receptive hearts and open arms. It is something to lose our lives for in order to find our lives (words of Jesus recorded in all four Gospels).

We are like those disciples who encounter the risen Jesus while trying hard to fish one morning, using the skills they had developed before they ever met Jesus. Their experience and expertise get them nowhere. Jesus tells them to cast their nets on the other side. Their three years with Jesus have taught them the

RENEWALS

wisdom of doing what he says to do, even if it seems to make no rational sense. They obey, and, well, you know the rest of the story (John 21:1-6).

The knowledge and experience of our past may not serve us for the future to which God is calling us. We may need to cast our nets into riskier water, into the deep flow of yet unknown love, into the mystery. There we will discover the depths where God is drawing us closer to himself, to others, and to the next step of our journey.

Dear Lord, I await a message from your heart to mine. Help me to see and confess any pretense in my living that is an exaggeration, if not, a lie. I ask your Holy Spirit to weaken my pride in preparation to receive what you will reveal to me and then ask of me. Amen.

June 21
A Covenant of Life Together Forever
Scripture for Reflection: Luke 24:13-50

In his last covenant-making appearance to Abram, God says, "Walk with me and be trustworthy" (Genesis 17:1b). This invitation to a more intimate, shared journey with God is new. Earlier, the calling was to travel and claim a new place as God's gift. Now the calling is to walk with God as a trustworthy partner. His name Abram ('exalted ancestor') will be changed to Abraham ('ancestor of a multitude') (v. 5). No longer is his call to prominence; it is now to walk with God and to father a covenant-keeping people. It is a calling to share life together with God and God's people.

You will remember the appearance of the resurrected Jesus to the two men on the road to Emmaus. The two are mourning the death of Jesus, their Rabbi. When Jesus appears alongside them, he is not recognized, but they are surprised that he does not seem to know of the crucifixion. They see what has happened as a terrible tragedy for the movement of which they are a part. They are shocked when *he* now starts explaining to *them* how what has happened falls in line with much of what the prophets said would happen. Who *is* this traveler?

They don't fully recognize him until they share the intimacy of a meal with him. When he, the stranger and guest, surprisingly assumes the role of host—taking the bread, breaking it, and sharing it with them—they realize who he is. Their eyes are opened and their hearts set on fire. Death has not taken Jesus from them; it has made him present and available. His death has become the doorway to resurrection. This encounter is more than a brief but spectacular glimpse of Jesus. It is the sign that he is now everywhere, accessible, and sometimes almost visible on their road to tomorrow; and he seems especially present where two or more are gathered.

What begins in Scripture as a calling of one person, Abraham, to walk with God in faith and to raise up a people to do likewise, now becomes *a universal calling*. The resurrected Christ calls us to raise up a new people who walk alongside him in the promised land that is the whole world. Wherever we live and work, he calls us to walk with him. We don't need to summon him; he's already present. We can see and believe in him through the eyes of faith, as the two Emmaus travelers did. Then we can walk with him for the rest of our lives and throughout eternity, loving him and learning from him how to walk and talk in a new way.

The story of the Emmaus encounter continues with the two disciples rushing back to Jerusalem to share the news with the other disciples, who by now are almost convinced of Jesus' resurrection. And then Jesus appears. Sensing their fear, Jesus identifies himself by showing them his crucifixion scars. Much relieved, they share fellowship and food. Jesus tells them that what has happened is fulfillment of the Law from Moses, the prophets, and the Psalms.

And then he sends them out "to all nations" (Luke 24:47c), to know "the only true God, and Jesus Christ, whom [he] sent" (John 17:3). Today, we do this as the early church did—as

Christ's Body. We do it together for the rest of our lives on earth, walking with God and his community of faith, day by day together, toward the future we share—eternity with the Trinity and our fellow travelers. All of us together forever.

"Look! God's dwelling is here with humankind. He will dwell with them, and they shall be his people. God himself will be with them as their God. He will wipe away every tear from their eyes. Death will be no more. There will be no mourning, crying, or pain anymore, for the former things have passed away." Then the one seated on the throne said, "Look! I'm making all things new" (Revelation 21:3b-5a).

Loving Lord, please show me how to walk with you together with my fellow Christian travelers, today and forever. In your name, Jesus, Savior and fellow traveler. Amen.

OUR CHURCH COVENANTS

June 22

Joining the Family

Scripture for Reflection: Ephesians 4:11-16; Philippians 1:27-28a

The Xhosa people of southern Africa have a saying that can apply to both the necessity and value of the church for any Christian: "*I am because we are.*" That may not sit well with many in this age of extreme individualism, relentless personal driven-ness, and addiction to winning out over all competitors; but it is truth for any follower of Jesus. Christians simply cannot do without the Body of Christ. We can even say that our conversion to Christ is not complete, or is not being completed, until we join Christ's family, the church—or to adapt the Xhosa saying, "I am able to live as a follower of Jesus because of his faith community where I am a member."

Another way to say it is that church is our spiritual home on earth. The family we grew up in may have given us a good start on the Christian way, or it may not have. We may have some Christian friends we occasionally share fellowship with, or we may not. The church is different still. It is not confined to a group of people related to us or just like us, people we are comfortable with. You will remember that time and again the New Testament church had to address the exclusions by one group or another based on religious background or social status. My own church

RENEWALS

(The Salvation Army) was so set on being an *inclusive* Body of Christ that many of their earlier congregations placed above the platform at the front of the chapel a large banner or painting that said in emphatic King James language, "Whosoever!" Whoever desires may come to this family gathering and be welcomed by both Christ and his family.

When we become a part of Christ's family on earth, we're giving up certain things. We're giving up our preference to associate only with people we naturally like or feel comfortable with. We're giving up the freedom to get lost in the crowd and keep everything to ourselves. We're giving up a faith that is self-centered, private, and overly cautious. But consider what we're gaining. We're gaining the great joy and challenge of being with those Jesus himself chose to be with: the outsiders, the people without confidence in their unassailable righteousness, the humble in spirit. We're gaining confidence in being with people we never thought we could connect with. We're gaining fellowship with people, some of whom are growing in genuine holiness because they confess their shortcomings and their sins. They know they are not perfect, but they are moving in that direction. They may not be able to articulate their faith eloquently, but they are learning to live it and to take their important place in the Body.

Think of your church as a family meal to which you're drawn because at this table we receive Christ's body, broken and sacrificed for us. He shares the cup of his covenant, his saving blood poured out over the whole world. Here we become one community in Christ, a covenant community, founded on a cross, a resurrection, and a Holy Spirit Pentecost. A community transformed by incomprehensible, all-inclusive love. A community of people who see each other through to God's future.

Peter De Vries was a satirical novelist who focused on writing novels in which religion played a major part. Raised in the church, he was well-acquainted with the flaws and foibles of the religious, and his writings exposed them. But something he once said ironically captures why we come together as this family of God called church: "We are not primarily put on this earth to see through one another, but to see one another through."

As members of Christ's Body, his church, his family, we learn to trust each other by being trustworthy ourselves. As our faith in Christ and our love for each other grow, we help each other through—all the way to the end, which is the beginning.

> *Loving Lord, help me to be a trustworthy member of the congregation where I worship and am discipled. Give me the courage to reach out to someone I trust when I need a fellow traveler to help me through. And please grant me your compassionate vision to see others who need some help through a tough place. I ask in your caring name. Amen.*

June 23

Joining the Choir

Scripture for Reflection: Psalm 40:1-4; Ephesians 5:18-20

My wife Keitha and I enjoy singing in the choir of our church. In our denomination, the choir goes by the name "songsters," a term we rarely hear outside The Salvation Army. One of the definitions of a songster is 'a bird that sings.' Keitha is an unabashed bird lover, and she happens to be a professionally trained singer as well—lyric coloratura, to be exact. Our songsters consist of musically-endowed singers at one end and songsters less so (like me) at the other. Our songster leader Daniel drills us on the details of the music: our blend, harmony, expression, and rhythms. But those disciplines, as important as they are, are not the bottom line. The bottom line is for us to be so captivated by the sacred music that the congregation will fall captive to it as well.

"[The Lord] put a new song in my mouth,
 a song of praise for our God.
Many people will learn of this and be amazed;
 they will trust the Lord" (Psalm 40:3).

A church choir can be a very good model or version of what a church is called to be. Each choir member is unique in the range and quality of their voices, as well as the level of musical gifting and training. Each member is also unique in spiritual experience and maturity, psychological makeup, age, and appearance. The calling of that choir is to integrate this rich diversity to sing this one song that will cause the church to listen and be drawn into the invitation. The best sacred music hypnotizes us with irresistible melodies and luring harmonies. "The bird sings," says Anthony Demelloy, "not because it has a statement, but because it has a song." It is the song that draws us. We sing, as do the birds, because music has its own charm, and if we can get the choir to blend their voices together in song, the congregation may just get the message.

Perhaps in our day of divisions and labeling, the church needs to sing songs that lure us into unity under the spell of Jesus. As our and many other nations are divided from within, so are Christians. The tragedy is that personal, social, and even political divisions are so often brought inside the church and become the basis of judging and isolating one another. Also, our inability to share our positions without judging the positions of others keeps us silent about 'those things we dare not talk about.' The willingness to listen to one another, rather than labeling, is God's gift. Like a choir, the church as a whole is called to take the diversity of its members and through the love and grace of our Lord and plenty of practice, blend it into sacred music.

Like a sacred choir, the church is called to sing in the freedom of the Spirit (1 Corinthians 14:15b); to sing and make music to the Lord in their hearts, even to communicate with one another through songs, hymns, and spiritual songs (Ephesians 5:19); to sing, not just speak, their gratitude to the Lord (Colossians 3:16c); and to give witness to the world by singing praises to God's name (Romans 15:9d). All this paves the way for the "new song" they will sing throughout eternity (Revelation 5:9a). Our songs unite us as a Body of Christ and as a people called to sing our Savior to the whole world.

All of us might not be ready or able to sign up for the church choir. But we all are called to live like a sacred song. A song that needs no singing skill. Only a singing heart and the compelling sounds of a life transformed by God's love.

Dear gracious God who sang us into existence, I ask you to tune me to the Body of Christ of which I'm a part, so that my contribution will point to the melody of your saving grace and contribute to the rich harmonies of your love. I pledge myself, through your empowering Spirit, to practice my part to help your church become a work of your art, through Jesus. Amen.

JUNE 24

LOVING EACH OTHER

Scripture for Reflection: John 13:34-35

We cannot love another human unless there is another human to love; so, God created a second human (Genesis 2:18, 21-23). But God didn't stop there. He created a third (with the cooperation of the two); from there on, the growth of the human race was exponential. The numbers one, two, and three are important in the story. They send the message that we humans were created to be a community. Not loners. Not even only a couple. (Any couple, whether a friendship or a marriage, can become so obsessed with and lost in their own relationship that they have little love and energy left over for anyone else.) God created us so that he could love us, we could love him, and we could grow that love in all our relationships with others.

God's love builds communities and thrives in communities. Within God, love is expressed in the community of Father, Son, and Holy Spirit—the Trinity. In the world he created for us, his love takes the form of our love for him expressed concretely in our love for each and every other. Much of society in the world of the apostle John was a cesspool of hatred, as is our world today, sadly. In his first letter to the church, John acknowledged the fact that Christians were hated for following Jesus; and then he said that their love for each other was the path to life, as hatred is the path to death (1 John 3:13-14). American novelist Thornton Wilder closes his Pulitzer Prize winning novel, *The Bridge of San Luis Rey*, with a sentence that has lingered with many readers since the book first appeared in 1927: "There is a land of the living and a land of the dead and the bridge is love, the only survival, the only meaning" (HarperPerennial, 1955, p. 107). According to John's Gospel, Jesus added a new commandment for his followers: "Love each other. Just as I have loved you, so you also must love each other" (John 13:34). In this world of exploitation, purposeful exclusion of others, and hatred-driven intolerance, love can only be nurtured in an intentional community of compassion. The church is that place; it is where we give ourselves in love to Christ and to each other. And as we do so, albeit imperfectly, we reveal Jesus of Nazareth to the world and ourselves as his authentic disciples (v. 35). In other words, the church we attend, our spiritual family, is where our Christian credibility must be grown. It is our firsthand school for learning the transformative power of Jesus' love. Love each other as I have loved you, says Jesus. "Keep loving each other like family," says Hebrews 13:1.

Perhaps a major contributor to the largescale defections from Christianity over the last hundred years has been our failure to be the church for which Christ gave his life to make possible. Too often, people see a church populated by people who demean each other and despise those who aren't like them. The Body of Christ is no place for haters; though truth be told, we have moments when Christ's love does not prevail in our lives. The church, however, *is* also a place for confession and forgiveness. Thank heavens! Her members will not be Christ to each other by pretense. Rather, they will do it by the seriousness of their pursuit of Christlike love and their honesty about when they fall short. Humbled by love, they make more room for Christlike love.

Christ's love is a bridge to be crossed, from the land of our sin and failures, the land that leads to death, to the land of the living, which is eternal life in Christ Jesus our Lord (Romans 6:23). We travel it in the company of our brothers and sisters in Christ, who love, support, and look out for one another. Our very nature is to cross the bridge together. It's called the church.

Loving God, as I daily cross the bridge from death to life, the bridge to love's eternity, please help me to give love generously and receive love graciously as part of your Body on earth. I ask in the name of Jesus, your incarnate Son and our loving Savior. Amen.

JUNE 25

SHARING THE WONDER

Scripture for Reflection: Acts 4:32-35

Keitha and I were relaxing one recent evening in front of the TV. There was nothing that appealed to us listed on the TV Guide. We had just watched the news and were now allowing the TV to remain on the same channel. The new program was musical—you know, the one where grey-haired musicians sing popular songs from the past to a grey-haired audience, who dearly love and are now lip-syncing the words while tears roll down their cheeks. Honestly, we don't usually watch these programs, but that night we were too tired to resist. One of the singing groups was a white-haired man with a guitar and two white-haired ladies. Suddenly, Keitha sat straight up in her seat and exclaimed, "The lady on the left looks *exactly like Mrs. Zink!*"

"And who is or was Mrs. Zink?" I asked. I had never heard Keitha mention her. "She was my third grade teacher at Roosevelt Elementary School!" said Keitha, as if I should know. Keitha's gratitude and obvious love for this lady was unmistakable. The subject was birds. Mrs. Zink loved birds, and eight-year-old Keitha had begun to love them but didn't know a lot about them. Having nothing to do with what she was paid to do as an elementary school teacher, Mrs. Zink announced to her class that she would be at the Jersey Meadows at 6 a.m. for those of her students who wanted to learn more about wild birds and obtained parental permission for the excursion.

Keitha was completely taken in by the magic of meadowlarks, upland plovers, towhees, red-winged blackbirds, and other bird species the Meadows would reveal on those hikes. She took the maximum number of visits her teacher offered per person. Keitha was hooked for life. Her love for birds has never wavered—all because a schoolteacher invited those who were curious about the mysteries of God's feathered creation to experience the wonder personally.

I wonder if Mrs. Zink's passion to explore the deeper wonders of God's natural world and then share it with others is akin to something we followers of Jesus are called to discover in ourselves: a passion to experience and then share multiple expressions of the beauty of God, which many people know little or nothing about. Are we, who are discovering the love and grace of God in our own lives, not called to expose someone else to the miracle?

You may not be a biblical scholar, or you may feel awkward as a spiritual guide for others. Be at peace, the qualifications lie elsewhere. They lie in what you know because you've witnessed the ways of God; you've seen divine miracles and have been one of those miracles yourself. You are still on the way, in the company of Jesus and of a group of fellow travelers called church, each member reaching out to one another for spiritual insight and support on the journey. Those helping relationships are acts of love where we share with one another the ever-new wonder and wisdom God has granted us.

Mrs. Zink was a highly effective guide because she knew her subject and was so passionate about it that she inconvenienced

RENEWALS

herself to share the wonder with third graders, at least one of whom I know still lives in the wonder of that world. In the world of the Spirit, you and I are privileged to pierce barriers of ignorance and share our discoveries with others and, at the same time, to open our own hearts and minds to what others can reveal to us.

Dear Jesus, Lord and Guide of my journey, give me the passion to share the discoveries of my spiritual journey with my fellow travelers, and the humility to draw help from the treasury of your grace in their lives. May I never outgrow the wonder of your generosity, which it is my privilege to share with others. In your name, amen.

June 26

Being Christ's Bride

Scripture for Reflection: Matthew 22:1-10

In this month of weddings, let's consider that one of the most intriguing names for the church is 'the Bride of Christ.' The prophet Hosea imagines the people of God (Israel) as a corporate bride called to be faithful to her husband (God). The image is a painful one for the prophet because his own wife Gomer, a former prostitute, has abandoned him for other lovers. He can identify with the pain God is feeling. He also has prophetic insight; he knows that, like a loving husband, God will not abandon his Bride, his people. Nor can Hosea abandon the wife who deserted him. He will find her and "speak tenderly to her heart," and "give her a door of hope" (Hosea 2:14-15), just as God will pursue Israel, not like a false, corrupting master (Baal) but like a loving divine husband who will honor the marriage covenant he has made with her (vv. 16-18).

In the New Testament, the metaphor of a marriage or a marriage feast is used in both the first three Gospels and the concluding Book of Revelation. Matthew, Mark, and Luke record the time when Jesus was asked why John's disciples and the Pharisees practiced the discipline of fasting and Jesus' disciples didn't. In answering the question, Jesus uses the analogy of a wedding feast where he is the bridegroom and his disciples are the guests. His three-year ministry on earth is, if you like, the ongoing recruitment of wedding guests (disciples). The time to fast will be when he, the groom, will be taken away from his disciples, the Bride (Matthew 9:14-15). In Luke's Gospel, the wedding feast metaphor is also used by Jesus to describe his invitation to enter the kingdom of God. Those known personally by the host turn down the invitation. As a result, the host invites just about everyone else, the ones you'd never think would be invited. This image of unlikely guests being not only invited but *qualified* to become full participants in the kingdom-of-God marriage feast is the scandal of the gospel! It is yet another expression of the upside-down character of the church compared to the normal social order. Christ's divine preference for "the least of these," who tend to be among those who acknowledge their unworthiness to be invited.

Seeing the church, or our own congregation, as preferring those who aren't preferred in the world at large is strange and for many, objectionable. We certainly want respectable people in our church—some good tithers, solid citizens, etc. Yes, so long as we never forget that Jesus preferred the company of so-called lesser people—the poor, outcasts, and self-professed sinners. He seems fine—in fact, happy—to enjoy fellowship with a Bride (a church) whose members don't look impressive on the outside and may even have a checkered past. As for some we may consider religiously upright, Jesus has this uncomfortable habit of exposing the sin that so often lurks beneath impressive successes and pious exteriors.

In Revelation, we get a glimpse of Christ's Bride. They "have come out of great hardship. They have washed their [sin-marked] robes and made them white in the Lamb's [Christ's] blood"

(Revelation 7:14b). Then, in chapter 21, we see John's vision of "a new heaven and a new earth" (v. 1). God has come to dwell forever with his people. The Bride of Christ (the church) is here transformed into the New Jerusalem, a city with no temple because "it's temple is the Lord God Almighty and the Lamb" (v. 22). And by grace, we, the lowly, all-of-us, fall on our knees and worship.

Lamb of God, Savior, we thank you for the privilege of being a part of your church, your Bride. Help me to give her the honor she is due. Keep me from using her for my own purposes. And give me the grace to humble myself before all my fellow members. Amen.

JUNE 27

LOVING THE CHURCH

Scripture for Reflection: Matthew 16:18; John 17:20-23; Colossians 2:1-2

Most Christians have fallen in love with Jesus. But falling in love with Jesus' Church, his Bride, his Body on earth, is a different matter it seems.

Some congregations are hard to fall in love with. Their traditions may have grown stale and lifeless with little sense of the original purpose. Unfortunately, church traditions can become ends in themselves, practiced as religious obligations, but divorced from the very purpose for which they were brought into being. When Paul tells the church at Thessalonica to "stand firm and hold on to the traditions we taught you…" (2 Thessalonians 2:15), he is referring to honoring the fire those traditions were designed to ignite. He is telling this church to embrace practices he has taught them as ways to see into the loving heart of God, to open their own hearts to this radical love, and to begin to see how they can live out this love in the world where they live. We can begin to fall in love with church when we risk understanding and then living by the real purpose of its traditions. And if a tradition is long dead, perhaps a new one is called for.

Some congregations are difficult to love because they have their fair share of differences and squabbles that we don't want to be a part of. Or, they may have members whom we're afraid we would have trouble relating to. No church congregation is perfect. Indeed, to greater or lesser extents, they all have their fair share of differences and squabbles. We only need to read from the Book of Acts through to the end of the New Testament to realize that the kinds of flaws and failings that developed early on have persisted in one way or another to this day.

The New Testament letters that are written to specific churches sometimes call for an acceptance of differing viewpoints or convictions. This can be seen in the way Paul addresses the issue of whether or not Christians should eat food offered to pagan idols. He says to follow one's own convictions in the matter without judging those who think otherwise (1 Corinthians 8). We also see a drawing of the line where certain views or behaviors are not in keeping with the way of Jesus. Consider Paul's assault on the false premise of certain reactionary members who are dismissing the adequacy of gentile conversions by insisting that they are not complete without obedience to certain Jewish rituals and practices (Galatians 3:1-5, 26-29; 5:1). Divisive issues may also relate to long-standing feuds, conflicting ambitions, or lack of focus. Or the diversity of the membership may present challenges the congregation will need time to resolve.

The fact that the New Testament churches all seemed to have issues that needed to be addressed tells us something important: in no congregation does *everything* go along smoothly all the time. Sometimes church is messy. If we take seriously the call of Jesus to be an inclusive church, the differences and prejudices within a congregation will inevitably precipitate some misunderstandings, and perhaps, confrontations. The calling of every congregation is to trust the reconciling grace of our Lord Jesus to bring unity out of division and diversity. By the grace of our Lord, a Christian congregation can respect one another's differences and see and realize the unity that emerges from this mixed bag of people Jesus calls his Church, his Body, his Bride.

The love of Christ seems to work best in a congregation where members don't expect perfection from other members and aren't afraid to confess their own limitations and imperfections to one another. That kind of risk-taking, over time, will birth a church worth falling in love with, a church growing up into Christ, a church all Christians need.

Dear Jesus, thank you for gifting me with fellow travelers on the journey. Help me to see the church where I serve as my spiritual family, not perfect as I am not, but moving on together toward a holy maturity. Help us to help each other discover intimations of your grace in the Church you are building and we are falling in love with. In your name, amen.

JUNE 28

Coming Home to Church

Scripture for Reflection: Jeremiah 50:4-5; Ephesians 2:17-22; 3:14-21

Old and New Testament Jews celebrated homecomings in Jerusalem. As the psalmist said, "Because the Lord chose Zion; he wanted it for his home" (Psalm 132:13). "The Lord loves Zion's gates more than all of Jacob's houses combined" (Psalm 87:2). God did not confine himself to Zion, but for him there was something special and unique about it, something that touched his heart. It was the temple. It was the people. It was the history. It was true home.

So, the Jews had homecomings, huge reunions—pilgrimages, if you will—to and into Jerusalem, to reconnect with God, each other, their story, their identity, their spiritual family.

Today, many Christian churches have homecomings, some as often as once a year. Each one is connected to the story of that congregation. Those who have been a part of that story at one time or another are invited to come to honor the rich history of that church, to thank God for how this congregation nurtured their own faith, and to celebrate its witness and service to the community over the years.

About 2,000 years ago, there was a Jewish homecoming in Jerusalem that Christians have never forgotten. Some Jews whose families had migrated outside the Jewish homeland came back for Passover and Pentecost. They joined with home-based Jews who had become followers of Rabbi Jesus. During Pentecost, they were together in a large room when suddenly a loud wind swept through the place and individual flames of fire alighted on each one of them. Something holy was happening. Luke describes it as a Holy Spirit infilling. And, in retrospect, we recognize it as the birth of Christ's Church. And it happened at a homecoming.

You never know what's going to happen at a church homecoming when you connect with your spiritual roots, your history, your past identity, and maybe even your future. In our highly mobile world, we easily become disconnected from a church that formed us—a congregation that nurtured our young lives in the early steps of faith or steadied us when faith wavered in our early adulthood or deepened our relationship with Christ when life seemed devoid of meaning in the early or late middle years. We will always be a part of those churches because they were God's gift to us. They were not perfect, but they gave us what we needed at the time for our spiritual pilgrimage. They gave us a community where we experienced the presence and compassion of Christ. They were family when we needed a spiritual home.

We spend our lives on earth searching for home. We honor the families that loved us into reality, mentored our passions and gifts, accompanied us on the journey of faith, helped to form us as disciples, and stayed with us when we felt so alone. We may have strayed from our first spiritual home, or perhaps its message or ministry no longer spoke to our needs or answered the new questions that our lives then posed. The fact is that no church on earth can meet our every need or answer all our questions. A church can only invite us to be a part of the journey of Christ's family through the gifts of its graces and its blunders, its holiness and its confession of sins, its heights and its humilities, and its imperfect but growing love for God and one another.

Church is the family that God calls us all to come home to on earth. It is the family we need in to be a follower of Jesus. It is the family that has enough of heaven to keep us on track toward our eternal home, to our final homecoming, the forever and true family of God.

> *Dear God, thank you for Christ who became our Savior in Jesus, for your Holy Spirit who spiritually empowered a new Christian people, and for your Church, Christ's Body and Bride. Teach me to love your church, as weak as it sometimes is, so that its weakness may become strength and we become one family. I ask this in Jesus' name. Amen.*

OUR WORLD COVENANTS

June 29

Allegiance to God's Creation

Scripture for Reflection: Genesis 1:28-31

For these next seven days, our meditations will focus on *our relational covenants in the world*. Of course, these covenants are not disconnected from our relational covenants with God or with the church. How could they be since God is the Creator and Sustainer of the world, and the church lives its life and serves in the world? When we walk outside the door of our church, we realize that we live in a vast space called a community, a city, a nation, a continent, and a huge rotating globe called Earth. And we know this globe inhabits a vast and expanding region of other planets and stars called our universe—and beyond.

The Bible is quite clear that all of it is God's creation. In fact, Scripture speaks of the whole Earth praising God the Creator (Psalm 98:4-9), with heavenly planets and stars joining in as well (148:3). I'm told that the literal meaning of the word universe is "to turn around one thing." That one thing, we believe, is God, the Eternal Person, who creates it all and keeps it spinning.

For the time being, let's focus on that one small part of God's created vastness called Earth, the world we live in and are meant to be stewards of. It is a tragedy that so many people, and ironically many Christians, live their lives in the world as if their care and responsibility for it has little to nothing to do with the practice of their faith. One creation heresy goes back to the influence of certain Greek philosophers who separated the spiritual from the physical and devalued the goodness of creation. Some Christians live in such a way as to suggest that because they believe the physical has no lasting value, nature—including their own bodies—can be abused. Another creation heresy does value creation but only because of its potential for profitable exploitation. In the process of exploiting the earth for profit, we often fail to honor the gift by replenishing or renewing it.

What is the allegiance we owe to the earth? We know that God gave us this earth as a supremely good gift for both our survival (Genesis 1:28-31) and our enjoyment (Psalm 67). We honor the gift by cultivating it for the nutrition that we and the rest of the world need, and by protecting it from pollution and abuse. We honor it by moderating our high-speed lives so that we can stop and take in God's gift of nature's exquisite beauty and infinite variety. We also honor it by beginning to understand and appreciate the profound interdependence and unity of this complex planet God has placed us in.

We are a part of this earth. Without it, we don't prosper; we don't even survive. It is not only God's gift to us; we are God's gift to it. How, then, do we gift the earth? We gift it by *our stewardship of it*. The gift the earth needs from us is the gift of our caring. Our allegiance to it is our promise to God to treasure it and nurture it. It is to glory in it as a way to glorify its Creator, our always generous Lord. It is to confess that we are not finally owners, even though we may by the law of some government "rightfully possess" a bit of real estate. We are more privileged than that. We are God-appointed *stewards* of his creation (Genesis 1:28-31).

Perhaps we could slow down our urban pace from time to time. Walk in a beautiful park and notice every little beautiful form of life; or hike in a dense forest and let ourselves be overwhelmed by the majesty and durability of it. Sit beside a calm, clear lake and let its peace permeate our hearts and still our minds; or observe the waves in a strong wind and know that the winds make living things stronger. Perhaps we could even join the singing and dancing of all of creation worshiping before the altar of our Creator God—and then live our days in the glow and the gratitude.

Dear Creator God, thank you for placing us in a world of endless beauty and rich sustenance. Forgive us if we take any of it for granted, exploit it, or abuse it. If we overindulge ourselves of its bounty and by doing so deprive others, please convict and teach us the joy of enough and the poverty of too much. I ask this in the name of Jesus, who never wanted more than a modest enough for himself. Amen.

JUNE 30

ALLEGIANCE TO THE KINGDOM OF GOD

Scripture for Reflection: Matthew 6:9-10; Ephesians 3:14-21

"The irritating thing about the Bible—well, one irritating thing about it—" says Bill McKibben, "is that it keeps instructing us, in unambiguous terms, to do things we don't want to." The same thought may occur to us when we read through the four Gospels and try to take in everything Jesus said about what it means to live in the kingdom of God he was inaugurating. Does Jesus really expect us to pledge personal allegiance to *all* his teachings? Isn't that too big a stretch?

One thing we can say about Jesus' kingdom-of-God teachings is that they seem so extreme when compared to a normal, even somewhat respectable way of life. Perhaps the best word to describe them is to use the word "radical," in the sense of the *literal* meaning of the word: from the *roots*, the hidden part of the plant that determines what that plant is and shapes how it lives its life. In this sense, we can see Jesus' teaching about the kingdom of God in the Gospels as a way of living that's rooted in something deeper.

And what if that rooting was the love of God? Or God himself? Or something that flows unsparingly from his heart? The very thing that John's Gospel and letters never tire of informing us of. You know: "God so *loved* the world that he gave his only Son, so that everyone that believes in him won't perish but will have eternal life" (John 3:16, NIV). In his first Letter, John takes a big leap and goes even further. He says that God not only loves; he *is* love (1 John 4:7, 16b). The love is himself. He doesn't love because he makes a decision to love this or that person. He loves every person, as he loves the whole world he created. A song the children sometimes sing in my church opens with "You can't stop God from loving you." God doesn't sit down and debate whether or not to love any one of us. He can't help it. Love is who he is and, therefore, what he naturally does. He can't be stopped. At the very root of Jesus' teaching about living by the radical teachings of the kingdom of God is the very nature of God himself, Love itself.

God, in whom our life is rooted, is Love itself. We may feel we don't—or someone else doesn't—deserve God's love, but we or they can do nothing to prevent it. What we are privileged to do as his followers and imitators is to take the risk of allowing ourselves to be conduits of that radical love. This is what it means to live in the kingdom of God, the kingdom of this all-loving God. Every commandment that Jesus gave his followers is an act of love—loving God, loving one another, loving our enemies, giving hope to those who grieve and those without hope, coming alongside those who are hungry and thirsty for righteousness, showing mercy, seeking purity of heart, making peace, accepting persecution for the sake of righteousness, being harassed because of Christ—and the list of love actions to which Christ calls us goes on and on.

All these kingdom-of-God kinds of behaviors are certainly admirable, but we may not feel sufficient of ourselves to carry them out. We would be right to think that. Paul wrote something to the Ephesian church that helps us here:

> "I ask that Christ will live in your hearts through faith. As a result of having strong roots in love, I ask that you'll have the power to grasp love's width and length, height and depth, together with all believers. I ask that you'll know the love of Christ that is beyond knowledge so that you will be filled entirely with the fullness of God" (Ephesians 3:17-19).

Pledging our allegiance to the kingdom of God is having the faith to risk letting Christ live in our hearts. It is Christ deepening and expanding our love. It is Christ revealing to us the widths, heights, and depths of love at work in all its kingdom-of-God manifestations. And over the course of our lives, whenever we face a new challenge in our allegiance to a particular teaching of Jesus, Christ's Spirit gives us the power to grasp his love in this new way, as his love has grasped us.

Prayer suggestion: Take a few minutes to meditate on the three verses above. Then claim them in prayer and in your living.

JULY 1

ALLEGIANCE TO OURSELVES

Scripture for Reflection: Philippians 3:1-16

Among the most often quoted lines of Shakespeare are from his play *Hamlet* (Act I, Scene III). They are words of advice spoken by Polonius to his son: "This above all: to thine own self be true, /And it must follow as the night the day,/Thou canst not then be false to any man." Being true to oneself, however, requires or assumes that we know who we are. Today, many people change their identity as often as they change clothing styles. Others have no sense of who they are; or once did and have lost it. Some define who they are by joining hate-filled political groups premised on a race-based or others-dismissive culture. Still others have found personal identity in a church that requires unquestioning loyalty to a narrow-minded pastor and/or a set of legalistic and judgmental interpretations of Christianity.

In a world of lost, confused, shifting, and intolerant self-identities, how does the disciple of Jesus find his own true self to whom he owes allegiance? In the Bible passage for reflection above, the apostle Paul lists some of the outstanding accomplishments in his own religious life before he met Christ and everything changed. All his religious accomplishments as a member of the order of Pharisees suddenly became junk, garbage, throwaways. Paul is telling us we can be religious on the exterior while our inner self is dying of starvation.

So how do we discover our *true self*, the self that has been awakened and given life by Christ, the self that is not manufactured, invented, or pretended, the self that is worth our being true to? We must write off as loss our *false self*, says Paul, for the sake of Christ (v. 8). But it's not just a transaction, a tradeoff of a false self for a true self. Paul goes on to describe it as an intimate relationship with Christ his Lord, a knowing Christ that goes deeper than any other relationship. He says it's not any righteousness of our own, something we can manufacture, or that our self-produced 'goodness' can claim, not even our strict obedience to religious laws. Rather, it is the righteousness that comes from "the faithfulness of Christ" (v. 9) It is based solely on Jesus and the grace that he brought to us, the grace that wins us over and empowers us to give up on our false selves, our pathetic accomplishments, our empty assets, and live by faith in him.

Jesus *is* our true self. He comes to us as a beacon of our true identity. He is the image of God in the flesh, shedding light and clarity on who we are as those whom God created in his image. As different as we are from each other, Christ gifts us all with his image, the Godlikeness that makes us truly human. It comes from knowing Christ, receiving the power of his resurrection, participating in his suffering, being conformed to his death, and reaching the goal of the resurrection that follows death. It is not won by our self-conscious spirituality; it is pure gift, received only by faith (Ephesians 2:8-10).

Once we have said and believed this, we have nowhere to go except to our knees, the place where we confess our utter helplessness without Christ, the place where only our humbling gets us anywhere worth going, the place where we're ready to receive the marks of our true identity, the marks of Christ. Here, and here alone, is where we find our true self. So long as we remain here, we have an identity, a self to which we can be true and give allegiance.

Father, Son, and Holy Spirit, as you have chosen to bind my identity to yours, please help me to surrender my false identities to your grace, so that I can more and more gain Christ, be found in him, know him, participate in his life, be conformed to his death, and be transformed by his resurrection. May this relationship, this imprint, by your grace reveal in some way my allegiance to the better me you are making. In Jesus' name, amen.

JULY 2

ALLEGIANCE TO OUR FAMILY

Scripture for Reflection: Deuteronomy 5:16; Luke 2:41-50

Having allegiance to the family that raises us or the family we raise requires that we have some understanding of what God has in mind by placing us in families. Someone has said that parents have two gifts to give their children: *roots and wings*. That seems to me a good summary of the essential tasks of a family. When parents, or a parent, give children both these gifts, they have done well. When parents focus overwhelmingly on the rooting and discourage their children from forging their own paths, self-trust and confidence may become difficult as the child matures. On the other hand, when parents don't provide direction and meaningful purpose, children may become trapped in aimless wandering from one pursuit to the next.

When I look back at my own upbringing, I can see clearly that my father wanted to see me well grounded in my faith; my mother trusted where my faith journey would take me. He didn't want me to stray too far in my thinking; she didn't want me to feel too confined. In some families, however, it's the mother who gives the rooting and the father the wings. In still others, only one parent gives both, and in others little of either is given.

We are not finished with our need for a family when we graduate and go off to a job or a college. We all continue to need relationships and groups that deepen our roots and strengthen our wings. We need mentors and support groups. So, we adopt new families, as it were. Some people don't find a good family until they leave and find the nurture and grounding they didn't get at home.

What does it mean, then, to have allegiance to our family? No family is perfect. We may idolize our family, but such a profile is seen only through rose-colored glasses. We can appreciate how good our family is only if we know its shortcomings, which makes its graces and its strengths stand out all the more. Some families are rife with dysfunction and abuse. Those who grow up in such families often reach out to surrogate parents or siblings and find the nurturing and companionship they lack at home. Perhaps over time they come to understand that their parents were fighting personal demons and were themselves victims of instability and abuse.

Jesus had a high view of the family. Raised in a very good family himself, he was taught the ways of God and the life of godliness. He emphasized the importance of honoring our parents (Mark 7:9-13). But when his calling required him to abandon his carpenter work, he had to do so without their full understanding and support. His mother seems at first to have thought he was making a big mistake (Luke 2:48).

Our family, whether the family into which we were born or a surrogate family, is God's gift if it gives us both roots and wings. Without the roots, we are lost and must find a grounding somewhere; without the wings, we are stuck and must find the courage to seek the unique calling for which we were created. The purpose of the family that follows Christ is for members to help one another be both grounded in Christ and free in Christ.

RENEWALS

As imperfect as our family may be, we owe them a certain allegiance, as stated in the fourth of the Ten Commandments (Deuteronomy 5:16), even if we had to find better families. And as perfect as we may consider our own family to be, it must not become an object of our worship. We worship only God, and among the graces he grants us are families who—more or less, but always to some extent or even in strange ways—are conduits of a measure of that grace.

Loving God—Father, Son, and Holy Spirit—in the spaces between the imperfections of the families I belong to, help me to see undeniable touches of your grace and love, beautiful reflections of your threefold, perfect life. In the name of Jesus, amen.

JULY 3

ALLEGIANCE TO OUR CHURCH

Scripture for Reflection: Philippians 1:3-11

In the eight meditations from June 21 to 28, we reflected on our calling to be a part of the Body of Christ, the church. Today, we will grapple with the question of what our allegiance to the church where we attend looks like, especially in light of the fact that no church on earth is perfect.

The New Testament is clear that our lives as Christians must be negotiated within the specific Body of Christ on earth we call church. We have seen how essential the church is for any Christian. But how do we separate the wheat from the chaff, so to speak, to claim and focus on what is essential to our church's calling, the things that really do deserve our full allegiance?

All Christian movements that become churches or denominations develop traditions designed to preserve the original purposes of the movement by continuing the practices that once advanced those purposes. Often, the traditions morph into something more settled, something less attentive to the original, more radical, life-changing purposes. Over time, the church (congregation) can become more complacent, satisfied with just the shell of a tradition. Spiritual stagnation sets in. Once-dynamic practices that fueled revival, spiritual growth, and mission now lack agency (people specifically committed to live them out in their lives) and allegiance (support from the congregation as a whole).

Christ calls us, his church, to become more than attenders, tithers, and sideline cheerleaders. He calls us to be a part of the church's calling: to meet together (Hebrews 10:19-25), to encourage each other (3:12-13), to carry each other's burdens (Galatians 6:1-2), to make sure there is no needy person in our fellowship (Acts 4:32-35), and to support one another as holy disciples of Jesus (Matthew 28:16-20). These are the graces that will prepare and equip us to live out our mission in the world. This is the kind of community that deserves our allegiance.

It is not for us who are church members, however, to take the easy path of standing by and criticizing our congregation for falling short of these standards. Rather, it is for us to humble ourselves and take the risk of stepping forward into this calling. To journey into a holiness that is authentic. To let the love of God inhabit us and overpower us. To be sold-out disciples of Jesus.

Practicing Christians are members of a church family that isn't perfect, as we are not perfect. Sometimes, says writer Brian Doyle, being a member of his church doesn't even make rational sense; it defies logic. It relies on this thing called faith, which means we're not in control. It leans on this thing called grace, this God-gift that opens us to miracles in, above, beyond, or outside our clever church planning. So why, asks Doyle, do I stay in my church?

> Where would I go that makes so little sense, that is so patently foolish, that could heal the bruised and bloody world, that could make a galaxy so crammed with light that it makes even its weary Maker smile, after all his work, that his children rose to their best selves, and sent

their sins wailing and gnashing into the limitless dark? ("Why I Stay in the Church," *Sojourners*, July 2014, p. 37)

Jesus entrusted his church to an unlikely, often clueless band of twelve, and the gospel thrived. It thrived because the cross and resurrection of Jesus, and the gift of the Holy Spirit, created a community with uncommon power to live out the self-giving love of God in the world. And they were able to do it, not with their cleverness, but with their reckless faith. A congregation that looks like that is worth the allegiance of its members.

Dear Jesus, help me by example to do my part to help my church family to be a faith-grounded, grace-filled, miracle-believing community worthy of allegiance and trust. I ask this in your name and for the sake of your church. Amen.

JULY 4

ALLEGIANCE TO OUR NATION

Scripture for Reflection: Matthew 22:15-22

In the second century after Christ, a Christian named Mathetes wrote a lengthy letter to someone named Diognetus. At one point, the writer, a more seasoned Christian, was trying to explain the Christian's relationship to the nation in which he lived. "Christians," he wrote, "live in their respective countries, but only as resident aliens; they participate in all things as citizens, and they endure all things as foreigners. Every foreign territory is a homeland for them, every homeland foreign territory." Within this paradox of in-but-not-of our nation, what does citizenship mean?

We all remember the now famous response of Jesus when his critics tried to trap him into saying something they hoped would get him into trouble with Rome. "Does the [Jewish] Law allow us to pay taxes to Caesar or not?" They were hoping Jesus, a Jewish messianic figure, would choose not paying taxes and maybe say something seditious to the effect that his new kingdom of God would overpower and replace the power of Rome. In response, Jesus rejected the legitimacy of the either/or premise and recast the question as a both/and. Showing the likeness of Caesar on the Roman coin used to make government tax payments, he declared, "Give to Caesar what belongs to Caesar and to God what belongs to God" (v. 21). And that was that.

Yes, paying taxes we owe according to the law of the land is the right thing to do. Professing Christians who hide money or find other ways to avoid paying the taxes they owe as citizens are, according to Jesus, failing their allegiance to their nation state. They are sinning.

There are other matters relating to Christians' allegiance to their government. A government many exceed the boundaries of its own legitimacy and act as if it were a god deserving of the total, unquestioning obedience of its citizens. This is precisely what the church faced in the first centuries of her existence. The Roman government murdered many Christians, but not because of their religious beliefs. They were happy for Christians to believe whatever they wanted to believe so long as they swore obedience to Caesar as the god above all gods. Christians said that *their* God, incarnate in Jesus, overruled all other gods, including Caesar, and obedience to Christ was non-negotiable. It is true to this day that a government may require its citizens to obey a law that for some violates a strongly held religious conviction. It wasn't that long ago that people were beaten and jailed, even killed, for refusing to obey segregationist laws that disobeyed God's law by dehumanizing fellow human beings.

There is another way in which a government can claim religious authority and presume to speak and act for God. Governments have taken the Christian community under its wing, granted it certain protections and privileges as the 'State Church,' forcing almost all citizens to be members of that established church and creating a spiritually weakened, nationalistic Christian culture. The state church then influenced government to outlaw certain beliefs and practices of other Christian movements, leading to shameful persecutions and imprisonments. Some of these non-conformist groups fled to America, where over time the government that was formed made freedom of religion and religious practice a cornerstone of the new democracy.

This separation of church and state has become an important component of the American political system. Government is constrained to respect our freedom to practice our religious beliefs so long as legitimate national laws are not broken. Presidents, legislatures, and courts are not to use their positions and powers to make decisions promulgating doctrines of religion.

This is good news for Christians! Followers of Jesus are strengthened in settings where the living of their faith is not forced by any government or state church. As much as a Christian loves the country of her citizenship, it must be a secondary love, subject always to her first love, which in extreme times may lead to civil protest or even disobedience. As much we love our nation, it is not our real home; our allegiance to it is superseded by a higher allegiance.

Dear Jesus, my one and only Lord, I thank you for the nation whose freedoms and protections I enjoy. May I never take them for granted. Give me the strength to stand my ground under your Lordship, even when my state government cannot support me. Give me the courage to stand up to that government when it asks of me what my loyalty to you doesn't allow. I ask this in your name and for your sake. Amen.

JULY 5
ALLEGIANCE TO THE POOR AND OUTCASTS
Scripture for Reflection: James 2:1-7; 5:1-6

When Julian the Apostate became Roman Emperor in 361, he set about to undermine the growing influence of Christianity by promoting the declining pagan religion to which he was devoted. He called Christians 'the Galileans' to emphasize that their religion was from a backward, unsophisticated extremity of the Empire. He was appalled, however, at the insensitivity of his own pagan priests toward the needs of the poor:

> "While (our) pagan priests neglect the poor," he wrote, "the hated Galileans devote themselves to works of charity, and by a display of false compassion have established and given effect to their pernicious errors. See their love feasts, their tables spread for the indigent. Such practice is common among them and causes a contempt for *our* gods" (italics added).

These Christians were simply living out an allegiance we find in both the Old and New Testaments. The prophets often railed against the excessive indulgences of the wealthy and powerful who were exploiting the poor and ignoring their suffering. Isaiah said that God would not abandon the poor but would respond to their needs (Isaiah 41:17). Allegiance to the poor was not an option for those who pledged allegiance to God. Serving God meant serving the least. The priority of care for the poor intensified in Jesus. Jesus' allegiance to the poor was proven by the excessive time he spent with them. He proclaimed in Nazareth that he had been sent to preach good news to the poor (Luke 4:18b). He said that God's kingdom belonged to them (6:20b), and in contrast, that the rich would suffer (6:24-25).

When William Booth left the Methodist ministry and, with his wife Catherine, relocated in the poverty-stricken East End of London, he chose the poor. One day, walking along the streets of that cesspool of degradation and suffering with his young son Bramwell, he said to the lad, "These are our people!" Years later he would say that he was "married to the poor" and must always be true to his Bride. His inner-city mission evolved into The Salvation Army and spread around the world.

Was Booth's allegiance to the poor intended for some and not others? Is it a special calling? Some people do have unique gifts for working with the disadvantaged. Should *they* be the ones to carry the responsibility of God's call to follow Jesus by "lifting up the lowly" and "fill[ing] the hungry with good things" (Luke 1:52b-53a)? The Letter of James is a stinging indictment of people of means being separated from the poor in church (James 2:1-4); for heaven's sake, "hasn't God chosen the poor as heirs of the kingdom he has promised to those who love him?" (v. 5b). Why wouldn't we want to get to know the true heirs and learn what they can teach us? The wealthy need the poor as much (or perhaps more) than the poor need the wealthy. Generously sharing resources with the poor from one's abundance is a cleansing. Scriptures clearly say there is no holiness for people of means without using their excess to combat the scarcity. They go even further: why not get to know the poor? Coming down from one's "prominence" to become friends with the underprivileged is a holy humbling that can change the heart of both the giver and the receiver.

Perhaps a comment of Walter Brueggeman in his book, *The Message of the Psalms*, best describes the real barrier to generosity. He suggested it's a lack of trust in *God's* generosity. If we believe God is stingy, or doesn't even exist, we're on our own. Everyone for themselves. Which is a pretty good description of where our world so often seems to be heading.

How deeply *do* we believe in the extravagant generosity of God? Deeply enough to imitate his generosity in our giving? Deeply enough to humble ourselves before the poor so that they can become our friends and teach us their wisdom? Deeply enough to share our table with them?

Dear God, lover of the poor and humbler of the rich, teach me the holiness of the common table and the beauty of barrier-breaking, inclusive friendships, so that I and others can become more and more like Jesus. I ask in his generous, loving name. Amen.

WEEK 6
SUMMER GIFTS

People of my generation will probably remember singer Nat King Cole's ode to summer. The song begins with an invitation to "roll out those lazy, hazy, crazy days of summer," and then proceeds to describe summer as the time of year for songs of cheer, picnics, locking up our home and getting out to the beach, romantic moons, and falling in love. And when it's all over, sadly "wish[ing] that summer could always be here." We're left with a vision of summertime as a carefree, sentimental escape from the rest of the year. The implication is that those other months are largely characterized by overwork and boredom.

Today, vacations are sometimes taken during other times of the year, especially for those who work in industries where summertime is when profits are the greatest, and those who can afford the air travel to warmer climates. For those who can afford it, summertime can be any time, especially when weather at home is damp and depressing.

I used to love our summer vacations when I was growing up. My parents would rent a place near a beach for access to swimming and where there were promising opportunities for fishing nearby. After Keitha and I married and were blessed with two nature-loving girls, we bought a tent, and for a few years enjoyed tenting vacations, mostly in the Appalachians. As the two girls were entering their early teen years, they let us know one day that they appreciated how much we enjoyed these camping-out vacations, but that, for them, the excitement had worn off. And that was the end of the camping. (Secretly, we were ready to end the roughing-it vacations as well!)

For most of us with more limited resources, vacation time extends no further than a month. Nevertheless, there is something about summer as a whole that may invite a certain thoughtfulness, a reflection on the future. It may be an opportunity to take the time to look at our lives in preparation for the next phase, or perhaps to wonder what will have changed or what needs to change. September or thereabouts seems to represent either a return to routine or the hope of a new beginning; and unconsciously or consciously, we may decide during the summer that some things will change.

In this week of meditations, we will explore the *gifts* of summer, the opportunities this season affords us on our spiritual journey. The changes we are concerned with are the changes that will help us deepen our relationship with God and strengthen our Christian witness inside and outside the Body of Christ. On July 6, we will discover how taking time off can become an opportunity to see God, ourselves, the world, and our calling in new ways. On July 7, we will see summer as a good time to consider taking a leap of faith by letting go of something in our lives and taking hold of something better for our future. On July 8, we will explore how this season can be experienced as a time of restoration and healing. On July 9, we will look at summertime as affording opportunities for solitude. On July 10, we will see the summer months as a time to reconnect with God. On July 11, we will encourage an openness to new discoveries and a willingness to take some risks that may bring us great delight and more spiritual depth. And on July 12, we will talk about re-entry—how we can bring these gifts of summer with us into the world in which we live year-round.

The real gifts of summer are not the escaping and the forgetting. They are the deeper pleasures of renewal and rebirth.

JULY 6

HOLIDAYS AND HOLY DAYS

Scripture for Reflection: Psalm 16:11 (NRSV)

*You show me the path of life.
In your presence there is fullness of joy;
In your right hand are pleasures forevermore.
(Psalm 16:11, NRSV)*

It wasn't that long ago that summer holidays as we know them were not, for most people, a regular part of the year's rhythm. People of means often escaped to their summer homes, where life was more leisurely and the atmosphere was healthier than in the city. The working classes had no such place to go and were fortunate to have a few days off for the summer. Save for the weather, summer for them was not that different from the rest of the year.

Much of this has changed. In the Western world, having paid summer vacation time is almost universally guaranteed for full-time employees. Think about that word "vacation." It comes from a Latin word (*vacare*) that means "to be empty or free." The emphasis is on being emptied of work responsibilities and worries that come with one's employment. A vacation is getting away, as it were, to another environment. In the UK, the term "holiday" is preferred to "vacation." Holiday is a modernization of an Old English word that meant "Holy Day." These were days when workers did not have to work because of an original association with a prominent day in the Christian calendar. The connection with specific saints and biblical events has been largely lost, but certain holy days remain national holidays. The irony is that they are still called holidays—holy days—although for the most part, they are not associated with the pursuit of holiness. For the great majority, they are simply designations for days off from work.

Many of our religious practices are scheduled in relation to the daily patterns and settings of each day of the week. As Christians, we look for intimations of God and opportunities to be witnesses in *all these settings*. In other words, *we are called to find the holy in every day*. The familiarity of daily patterns makes it easier to recognize the wrinkle or the unanticipated occurrence that may be a clue to God's invitation or intervention. A coworker who seems uncharacteristically quiet and sad may be a wrinkle that is God's invitation for us to reach out to him or her. Or our regular morning meditation may bring us to a Scripture passage that proves to be God's invitation to make a change that will have profound consequences for our future. Where we are more at home, we are better able to see the unusual revelations from God that get our attention.

What is the pattern of our Christian practices when we're on vacation? The days are different; following the same daily pattern may be difficult. We're in a new environment that is probably flooding us with new things. We enjoy ourselves in new ways. Our minds absorb the interesting unfamiliar at a fast pace. "Relax!", says a voice from beyond. "Your vacation is my gift for your pleasure." Yes, it's the voice of God, in whose

RENEWALS

right hand are pleasures forevermore! "Enjoy my gifts," he says.

Vacations are times of pleasure. Pleasure is not contrary to holiness unless it involves abuse of ourselves or others. C. S. Lewis puts the truth beautifully in one sentence: "Every earthly pleasure is an apprenticeship in adoration for the sort of thing that will go on forever in heaven." Maybe vacations are like playing heaven! So, let's not separate God from the pleasures of vacation. We can enjoy them as God's gift because he loves to give us pleasure, and our enjoyment of his gift gives him great pleasure, now and through eternity.

Dear generous God, we thank you for the pleasures of life you give us and especially for the holy days of summer we call vacation. Please free us to enjoy them, no matter how humble they may be, so that in the enjoying we may give you the pleasure of being our gracious God. We ask this in the name of the Son who gives you so much pleasure. Amen.

JULY 7

LETTING GO AND TAKING HOLD

Scripture for Reflection: John 21:1-8

For many of us, summer has been a time to take risks for which we had to prepare ourselves. For example, Keitha remembers at age seven being in the water, fearfully holding on to the dock at the deep end of Star Lake Camp. She was sure she wanted to be a real swimmer. To do so, she had to overcome her fears, let go of the dock, and swim all the way to the floating raft in the deeper water. She set off and did not turn back. She let go and took hold of freedom in the water and has been a superb free swimmer ever since.

She also recalls another summer day at the same camp when she, at nine years old, stepped across a line. The preacher was a man named Debavois. He told the story of the Alamo, where William Travis, facing his small band of fighters, drew a line in the sand and invited only those who were willing to fight to the end and likely die to step across the line. Keitha heard the tale in the mid-twentieth century, an era captivated by stories of real heroes. When Debavois drew a line in the sand of the tabernacle that night and invited all who would accept Christ as Lord of their lives (whatever the cost) to step across, Keitha crossed it and never turned back.

Keitha took another big step, this time with me, on June 22,

RENEWALS

1963—the day of our wedding in New York City. Both of us were petrified of the enormity of this life change, but we were ready to let go and take hold of a new life together for the rest of our lives.

Summer invites us to let go. It's a time to escape the repetitive schedules and work demands, relieve ourselves of some or most of the responsibilities that we carry from day to day, and focus on enjoying, even indulging, ourselves. Most do it with their family or a group of friends. It's a time to let go and have fun, as much fun as possible—vacation as a carnival of fun! Or for some, it may be something else. Perhaps a search for something new and demanding, like a hiking exploration on a challenging trail, perhaps one that requires strong physical stamina and an adventurous spirit. Or vacation might be something very simple: like doing nothing.

I think it would be fair to say that, for most of us, vacation is letting go of our normal routines and doing something refreshingly different. It's sad that some go on vacation in body but not mentally or emotionally. They just can't leave work. Their cellphones, still activated, are always nearby or on their person. They are, in their own minds, indispensable at their workplace. They can't let go. Their indispensability is an illusion, possibly just a need to be needed. Or it may arise from an intentional failure to prepare staff and build their confidence in keeping things going. The vacationer who can't let go has made sure he can't.

Letting go of our work is a liberating opportunity summer gives us. If our liberation was only temporary, however—a period of happy times followed by a return to our dissatisfactions when vacation is over—we have missed what's important. Letting go has a mission beyond temporarily relieving us of our worries or getting our brain to forget. It clears the way for a different vision, a better way to invest our lives. It may have given us a vision of something better to take hold of. Perhaps this is the leading of God, something about which we should pray and seek wisdom. If this is so, summer will have given us a substantial gift.

Along with our letting go may have come thoughts of taking hold of something new: a better way to serve, or lead, or minister, or work together, or use our gifts for God's kingdom. A summer break is a good time to consider and pray about such possibilities. If we sense God is leading us toward a more fruitful discipleship and service, and if we are ready to take the leap, we must prepare to let go and take hold, like disciples casting their nets in a new direction.

Dear Jesus, give me the vision to see the lines that you invite me to cross and grant me the courage to accept your invitation to cross over. I ask you also to give me the discernment to recognize and resist other invitations to cross a line to something that appears worthwhile but is only destructive to the soul. And precious Jesus, give me the strength to let go of anything in my life that is not worth clinging to and the motivation to risk taking some new step that may be uncomfortable to take at first, but more fulfilling and spiritually empowering in the long run. I ask these things in your name alone. Amen.

JULY 8

RESTORATION AND HEALING

Scripture for Reflection: Jeremiah 30:17a

> *I will restore your health,*
> *and I will heal your wounds,*
> *declares the Lord . . .*

    Even for those of us whose pace of life may not slow down in the summer, there is still something about those three months that can have a relaxing effect. Nature is in full bloom, making the world seem more inviting and welcoming. And, of course, there is that getaway called vacation. Maybe we relax and put down our guard a bit. Maybe we begin to think more about the direction our lives have taken and wonder what needs changing. Perhaps we know or sense that we've lost something and wonder if can be restored. Or we suspect our lives are not as healthy as we would like—spiritually, relationally, or physically.

    Summer is a good time to be attentive to our lives in ways that may be more difficult during the other, busier nine months of the year. Previous lack of attentiveness to our own needs may leave us with feelings of emptiness and a lack of deeper fulfillment. Perhaps God's gift of summer includes an atmosphere in which we can be less concerned about performance or success. We don't need to be on the defensive about ourselves. We can step back and, with the Spirit's guidance, take a closer look at our inner lives. Looking deeper, we may discover hidden needs or unfulfilled spiritual longings. We can confess these needs and express these longings to God and pray for his wisdom about addressing them. And we can explore Scripture for direction, and perhaps seek the counsel of a friend or mentor.

Summer invites us to lay aside our pretense and open ourselves to the God who can restore something important we may have lost over the year and heal the wounds we may have received or inflicted. The acceptance of our need for restoration and healing is not a sign of spiritual failure; it is a sign of spiritual integrity. It is another step toward the wholeness to which Christ continues to beckon us. At times, we all need restoration and healing. Summer is a good time to step back and seek it in the quietness, in a calmer, more peaceful environment, or with the presence of a spiritual guide or in the open spaces where God may appear unbidden.

I am amazed that Jesus usually did not accuse anyone who needed healing of being a sinner who needed forgiveness. He simply healed those who trusted him to heal by casting out the foreign, occupying demon (Mark 1:32-34). Neither did he condemn or dismiss those who recognized their need for restoration, as did Peter (John 21:15-17), whom Jesus forgave without needing to say so, only to speak proof of utter confidence in him: "Follow me" (v. 19b).

I have memories of summer camps during my teenage years where I was challenged and trained by camp staff to be attentive to my spiritual health and to be assured of God's restorative power when I failed him. I also remember summer nights during our tenting days when darkness descended and Keitha, Heather,

RENEWALS

and Holly usually went right to bed. I would sometimes sit outside reading a devotional book by the light of a small kerosene lantern, surrounded by a remarkable variety of flying insects that seemed to be joining in, as if God-sent. And in that mystic place, if you like, I felt God was restoring me, perhaps healing me as well. There is another summer event in August, a Bible conference sponsored by The Salvation Army at Lake Junaluska, North Carolina, that we attended most years throughout our adult life, and still do. Of the three speakers, there was always at least one who spoke words I needed to hear. And linking up with friends and colleagues was its own blessing and joy, the renewal of important life links.

Summer gifts us with enjoyment—and often with restoration and healing as well.

Dear loving Lord, I pray that along with the joys of this summer season, you will also grant me the restoration of anything of eternal value my soul may have lost and the healing of any wounds that may impair my life and witness. I pray in the name of Jesus. Amen.

JULY 9

SOLITUDE

Scripture for Reflection: Psalm 46:10a (NRSV)

"Be still and know that I am God!"

Heather Poxon, a Salvation Army officer, taught me a new word: *nomophobia*. It is the fear of having no mobile device. Paranoia over being without our mobile devices is almost pervasive, especially because these devices have become such a significant advancement in accessibility. Many are lost without them. Studies show that those who can't stand to turn their device off and who spend enormous amounts of time on it are increasingly removed from the realities of their immediate environment. There is a measurable loss of capacity or willingness to interact with discernment, empathy, or fairness to the people around them. Mobile devices have created their own worlds, and much of it is not only ill-informed and ugly, it is profoundly degrading. In my view, the more we are addicted to that skewed world, the further removed from Christ we become.

Heather has discovered one helpful way to combat the lure of cellphone addiction. She practices a discipline of cellphone abstinence for periods of time so that she can better connect with her immediate world. Her favorite setting for her engagement is the out-of-doors. The vibrancy, newness, and beauty of the natural world puts her in touch with the creativity and care of her ever-present Lord. I don't imagine that Heather is mowing the lawn or trimming the hedges during this time. She is probably doing nothing so that she can see God doing something; she is seeing, listening, feeling—opening herself to God at work in the world, not Heather at work. She is practicing *solitude* carved out by days or partial days (Heather Poxon, "Nomophobia and Nature," *The Officer*, Oct. – Dec. 2019).

Kalie Webb, also a Salvation Army officer, discovered a different way of practicing solitude during the course of her days. She calls them Selah Moments. The word "Selah" occurs numerous times in the Book of Psalms, usually to mark a break of some kind. Since the psalms were often sung, "Selah" could well have designated a break in the singing. At a deeper level, it seemed to identify a place in the psalm for the reader or singer to stop and meditate quietly on what the psalm had just revealed. In this sense, Selah is a time-out for deeper spiritual reflection. Kalie has applied this practice daily. She practices Selah at times when she is faced with something that invites her to stop and become aware of God or confront difficult circumstances that make her particularly aware of her need for God. It may be triggered by a sudden awareness of her desire to offer praise to God. She summarizes a Selah moment in four words: stop, pause, ponder, praise (Kalie Webb, "Selah Moments," *The Officer*, Oct. – Dec. 2019). Kalie is practicing *daily solitude* during her otherwise busy life. There are other ways to practice solitude. Making solitude part of morning Scripture reflection and prayer is one way; or as part of a retreat when we spend significant time alone with God is another.

"Solitude," said Henri Nouwen, "is the furnace of transformation.

Without solitude we remain victims of our society and continue to be entangled in the illusions of a false self" (Nouwen, *The Way of the Heart*, p. 25). I was a Christian for quite a while before I began to see my deep need for solitude. I started my solitude by practicing a quietness in my morning devotions where I simply waited until I sensed God's loving presence. I looked for his face. I listened for his voice—his assurance, his agenda, his correction, his forgiveness, his confidence in me, his healing. I then began to pray knowing that God was really there, helping me frame my petitions or telling me to trust his intervention, often without knowing exactly what it was. And in this time of solitude, he was inviting me to be free of my false self and become a person continually being restored in the image of Christ.

Why not take advantage of this beautiful time of year to discover solitude?

> *Dear God, restorer of my soul, steady my mind and calm my heart, so that I can contemplate your beauty, listen for your voice, seek your face, and submit to your will. Free me from my busyness and from any device luring me from my true self in Christ and from my calling to live in your presence throughout my day. I ask in Jesus' name. Amen.*

JULY 10

Retreats

Scripture for Reflection: Matthew 11:28-30

Calvin Coolidge, the thirtieth president of the United States (1923-29), once said, "Don't you know that four-fifths of all our troubles in this life would disappear if we would just sit down and keep still?" Baptist pastor Howard-John Wesley adds to Coolidge's homespun wisdom: "If you can't rest from it, you are ultimately a slave to it." It is quite possible, and more common than we may think, for followers of Jesus to be workaholics. They may wrongly see their overwork as what God expects of them, a measurement of their faithfulness. And Jesus says to them, "Come to me, all you who are struggling hard and carrying heavy loads, and I will give you rest" (Matthew 11:28).

Rest. God's gift to us all, and particularly to the workaholics. God's rest goes far beyond getting enough sleep, which some of us don't. It goes to the soul. It goes to what is happening *inside* us, to the growth of our inner life, to the journey within. Christians may think of their journey in life as how they live out their lives in the world, serving God and others. But what is the source of such a calling? Where is the depth from which flows the compassion, the mercy, the mind of Christ? How do we recognize Jesus in those we help and serve?

Yesterday, we talked about solitude as a pause from our activist life leading to a personal encounter with God. Why do some (possibly most) Christians struggle with this call to solitude? As an activist culture, we measure our effectiveness or success in terms of how much we get done. There is even a church hymn that has the line, "Let us labor for the Master from the dawn to setting sun." No wonder we become so weary in well doing. No wonder our spiritual lives so often get lost in the shuffle of 'good works.' No wonder our likeness to Christ is diminished in the distraction of our perpetual motion. No wonder what we do often outshines who we say we are.

Calvin Coolidge was right about one thing: practicing some stillness would solve a lot of problems. And Pastor Wesley was right: if we can't rest from our labors, we will become slaves to them. When Jesus invited would-be disciples "who are struggling hard and carrying heavy loads" to come to him for "rest," he is talking about more than a place for them to catch their breath or sleep the night. The word usually translated as "rest" can also be translated as "relief" or "a resting place." He is not giving us housing somewhere. He, the Giver, *is* himself the place he is giving us. And he is giving us the privilege of getting to know him well. And he is giving us his very different kind of yoke and burden: *his* easy-to-bear yoke and *his* light burden.

Jesus is teaching us that what makes our works *his* good works is our cultivation of a genuine relationship with him. The invitation he extended to his disciples to "come by yourselves to a secluded place and rest for a while" (Mark 6:31) was not only an invitation to recover from the hard work of their recently completed ministry; it was also an opportunity to spend personal time with their Lord. Think of Elijah, fleeing for his life, alone in that cave on Mount Horeb, finally hearing God, not in the sound of a powerful wind, or an earthquake, or seeing his presence in the fire. God came to him, instead, in a thin, quiet sound. Think of Jesus' forty days in the wilderness, fasting and praying in quietness, preparing himself to resist temptation and enter the work that lay before him. Think of the apostle Paul going to Arabia after his conversion, a three-year period of his life we know nothing about. Perhaps it was a retreat, time alone getting to know God in preparation for being Christ's spokesperson for the Mediterranean world.

God calls all his followers to a retreat, a quiet small place devoid of distracting noises and busyness, an environment conducive to hearing God and responding to his love. The retreat may be a regular daily appointment of half an hour or a more extended time of contemplation in God's presence. Whatever form it takes, it is a back-off from productivity and a step toward intimacy with God. These summer months can give us opportunity to practice retreating with God.

Dear Jesus, ever inviting me and waiting for me to be with you in the presence of the Father, please give me the discipline of sacred time with you so that I can become more like you and my work can vibrate with your presence and prove your love. Amen.

JULY 11
RISKS

Scripture for Reflection: Hebrews 11

Summer is an opportunity to go beyond the established patterns of our typical days and expose ourselves to the new: places, people, environments, outlooks, ideas. Summer gives us the opportunity to explore and advance our faith. The life of faith is always a journey beyond the comfortable habits of a more contained life, always a search both further and deeper. The best summer leisure is not so much a recovery from work exhaustion as the energizing of new discoveries in faithful living. Toward the end of C.S. Lewis's book, *The Last Battle,* Aslan—the Christ figure—invites the children: "Come further up, come further in!" Our summer leisure is a special opportunity to see beyond the confinements of our organized workdays and to imagine living our faith at greater depth in the presence of Jesus. It is a good time to contemplate a new risk—further up or further in—worth taking.

The Bible is replete with men and women who were called to go in a different direction or find faith at greater depths. Think of settled Abraham picking up stakes and moving his tribe to Canaan where he eventually became the father of a great Hebrew nation. Self-doubting Moses finally having the audacity to believe he could lead his slave tribe to escape from their powerful Egyptian oppressors and find the Promised Land. The prophet Jeremiah refusing to play it safe because he believed he spoke God's words. John the Baptist who told everyone, including those at the top, to get ready for the Messiah by renouncing and ceasing their sinful actions, and paying for it with his life. Christian martyrs following the example of their crucified Lord. These and countless others got outside their protected selves and risked a better calling. They are not presented to us as exceptions; they are presented as examples to follow.

Summer is a good time to practice solitude, retreat, and prayer, to go further up and further in. It provides us with signs of new life that can open us to a more substantive calling and a more fruitful spirituality. It gives us an extensive pause to assess our lives as disciples of Jesus.

Surrounded by the wonder of God's world, we see summer's ever-present growth and beauty. We see a world alive, the extraordinary miracles of our creative God; and we wonder what miracles God now wants to do in the lives of the creatures that we are. We see the power of the beauty around us, and we realize that the very same elements that comprise this extraordinary world are the elements we're comprised of. So, we ask, "Lord, what do you want to make of us with the raw material we are?"

During our summer leisure, we may meet people who inspire us in new ways and challenge our spiritual complacencies. Their lives may invite us to take new risks worth taking or to draw closer to Jesus in the quiet peace of our contemplations. We may discover mentors who can guide us in new directions or encourage us to take new risks in obeying our Lord. He or she may become our support for the risks we will take for Jesus.

Perhaps during summer free time, or at some other thoughtful time in the year, you have imagined taking some bold step forward in the practice of your faith. The step may be related to the depth of your prayer life, perhaps a challenge to invest in listening prayer and submission to Christ. Or the step may be related to the authenticity of your witness, perhaps a challenge to take more risks in the exercise of your faith in Christ. Whatever it is, Christ will honor your willingness with his approval and guidance. He will help you get over your fear of failure, and he will grant you genuine success so long as your self-confidence does not outweigh your humility.

Dear Jesus, who risked everything on me, please grace me with courage to risk everything on you. Strengthen the fiber of my love so that in your Spirit's strength I will allow myself the risk of loving you and all those you love, whom you have taught us is everyone. Help me to be present with you every day in prayer. Teach me in your presence to be quiet and to listen before I pour out my heart and make my requests. In the confidence of your guidance in prayer and the example of your life, I pledge that all I will do will be done in your strength. Amen.

JULY 12

RE-ENTRY

Scripture for Reflection: 1 Corinthians 2:9-13

Many people rely upon their past as the guide to their future. Indeed, we should learn from our past, especially from our mistakes and failures. But if we are captive to doing the same things that have given us a measure of approval and satisfaction in the past—if we are, as it were, being guided by the rearview mirror of our lives—we are living backwards.

God's summer gifts that we've been considering this week can be more than a temporary reprieve from business as usual. They can be a way into living a better future. God does not call us to be limited or even victimized by our past; he calls us to be empowered for living out our calling as his disciples in more fulfilling and Christ-honoring ways. We can learn from the past, but we must live toward the future.

We can experience the pleasures that God grants us, not just during summer vacations but throughout the year. Taking a day off each week is a restorative gift and a re-energizer of our calling. Such days are as holy as any other day, and each day is a part of the whole of our lives. "How you live [all] your days," says Annie Dillard, "is how you live your life."

We can convert the newness and excitement of what we experience during the summer into a willingness to take new steps, change old habits, even cross lines in the sand, because we see Christ ahead, calling us to it. He knows such change is not always easy for us. Often, it is hard to let go. We may have become attached to a practice that served our faith journey well in the past but is now failing to sustain or nourish it. The realization of this fact is Christ's gift, and it frees us to begin taking hold of a new future that is the substance of the gift.

Summer may also prove to be a time of restoration and healing. How do we take that home with us? The summer's restoring respite is not necessarily sustained, nor the healing necessarily complete. Successful re-entry will probably require the continuation of healing facilitated by commitment to healthy life patterns, the practice of Sabbath rest, and perhaps consultation from or mentoring by a trusted person.

Summers are good times to discover the gift of solitude. If we continue to practice the gift throughout the year, it will help our involvement in the world not to become entanglement. In the words of Henri Nouwen, "Silence teaches us to speak ... A word with power is a word that comes out of silence ... A word that is not rooted in silence ... sounds like a 'clashing cymbal or a booming gong' (1 Corinthians 13:1)" (*The Way of the Heart*, pp. 56ff). Even Jesus said that the words he spoke had been *given* to him by the Father (John 14:10). One of the most important life-changing experiences of our lives is the art of being quiet and letting God give us words.

Retreats are a good way to frame solitude. Whether the retreat is a half day, a full day, a weekend, or longer, if it takes place in a peaceful environment without invasion from the outside, and if we allow God to still our hearts and minds, it can be transformative. The word "retreat" is derived from an earlier French word that meant "a place of refuge." A retreat is not a place of escape. It is a place of safe refuge with God, a place to be present with God and allow him to minister to us and refresh our spirits, maybe even change our minds. Whatever resource we take—a Bible, a spiritual writing, or only our own readiness to listen—the important thing is our solitude and our readiness to submit ourselves to God.

A final gift that we need to take with us when summer is over is the gift of holy risk-taking. The saints of God do not take foolish risks, but they embrace the risks that Jesus asks them to take. Earlier we used the words C.S. Lewis put into the mouth of Aslan (Christ): "Come further up, come further in!" Christ continues to invite us to go further in our lives in the world as his faithful, courageous witnesses. And he continues to draw us closer and allow his Spirit to deepen us spiritually and strengthen our likeness to him. It's not for our lesser, careful selves; it's for those seeking the courage of Jesus.

Prayer suggestion: End today's meditation with a prayer that articulates your specific desire(s) and commitment for this next stage of your journey following Christ.

WEEKS 7–9
THE BLESSINGS OF THE BEATITUDES

How did certain sayings of Jesus come to be labeled "The Beatitudes"? The title we've given them was not present in the original New Testament manuscripts of Matthew 5:3-12 and Luke 6:20-23. It came from a Latin word, *beatus*, meaning "happy or blessed." Our English word "beatitude" means "perfect blessedness or happiness," and sometimes, "a blessing." It is a good title for the set of verses beginning with "blessed are" that we are considering in the Gospels of Matthew and Luke.

The word in the Greek New Testament is *makarios*, meaning "blessed," "fortunate," or "happy." Some modern English versions have abandoned the traditional translation, "blessed," perhaps because the word is rarely understood in our increasingly secularized world. "Fortunate," however, could describe something received by sheer luck or even a gambling windfall. It is also true, however, that a genuine follower of Jesus would feel fortunate to have received the undeserved saving grace of his Lord. And "happy" could suggest the feeling that comes with a temporary pleasure, a short-lived, even artificially induced emotional high. It is also true, however, that a follower of Jesus would certainly find deep joy in her relationship with him.

I am taking the view that "blessed" is still the best translation. My reason is this: each of the Beatitudes sheds a different light on what it *means* to be blessed. Each says something very specific about the experience of a true follower of Jesus. They all tell us the surprising qualities Jesus is looking for in us. Taken both individually and together, they encompass far more than the words "happy" and "fortunate" convey.

Traveling through the Beatitudes is not an easy trip. They are a high bar for those who dare to follow Jesus. The happiness and good fortune that each of them brings come at great personal cost. Think of the mother of Zebedee's sons coming to Jesus, pleading that he grant her two worthy sons the privilege of sitting on the right and left side of Jesus in his kingdom. Surely this would bring them fortune and joy. Jesus answers, "You don't know what you're asking! Can [they] drink from the cup that I am about to drink from?" (Matthew 20:20-22). The Beatitudes invite us to put the acts of self-giving love before the benefits.

Furthermore, the Beatitudes themselves are expressions of what is at the very heart of our lives as Christians: *living a holy life.* To be sure, holy living is another one of those biblical teachings that today is both misunderstood and misrepresented. Some reduce it to a legalistic straightjacket, which inevitably breeds judgmentalism and an uncaring separation from the world. Others see it as an impossible and, therefore, unrealistic way of life. The truth is that holy living, though it has its definite moral standards, is a way of life that is based on love and not law. It is living in captivity, without shame, to "the love of God that has been poured out in our hearts by the Holy Spirit, who has been given to us" (Romans 5:5). It is, as John Wesley said, moving toward love-based perfection, our God-intended human nature.

The Beatitudes are expressions of this love-based life. As all Christians are called to this holy living, so are they called specifically to beatitude living. Indeed, each beatitude expresses a dimension of the Christlike love to which God calls us all. This is not to say that all of them are our spiritual strengths or that they are all apparent in us all the time, although there are some Christians whose very lives undeniably shine a clarifying light on one or more of the Beatitudes. It is to say, however, that at a given time and place, any follower of Jesus may be in a situation where her call to holy living asks her to risk embodying a beatitude that she is not used to having to live out. For this reason, we take every beatitude seriously, even though by personality and preference there are some we must work harder at when the call comes. At those times, the witness we give has nothing to do with any claims we may make; it has to do with the depths to which we are willing to let God's love in Christ take us.

We usually identify "The Beatitudes" as the list of eight or nine beatitudes found in Matthew 5:3-12. Four of these beatitudes are approximately paralleled by four beatitudes found in Luke 6:20-23. In addition, Luke records Jesus delivering four 'woes' against those whose lives are the very opposite of his four beatitudes. Matthew's Beatitudes were given by Jesus in his sermon on the side of a mountain, and Luke's on a plain. Both accounts followed an extensive ministry of healing by Jesus. Both set the stage for the shockingly radical lifestyle Jesus' preaching was to outline and his life was to embody. The Beatitudes stunned his listeners, and both Gospels followed them with teaching after teaching that revealed a kingdom unlike any other.

A further comment needs to be made regarding these four similar beatitudes that appear in both Matthew's and Luke's Gospel. There are some differences in how those beatitudes are worded. Where Matthew has "poor in spirit," Luke simply has "poor." Where Matthew has "those who hunger and thirst for righteousness," Luke has "you who are hungry now." Where Matthew has "those who mourn, for they will be comforted," Luke has "those who weep now, for they will laugh." The fourth and final beatitude of Luke is about those who will be hated, excluded, reviled, and defamed on account of the Son of Man. They will rejoice in heaven. It is very similar to Matthew's ninth beatitude. Why the differences in the three beatitudes? Maybe it can be explained by the difference in the makeup of the crowd to whom Jesus was speaking. He may have adapted his message to the character and needs of the gathering before him. Or he may have been speaking more in general about the kingdom living of all his disciples in the Matthew Beatitudes ("Blessed are those who…") and more particularly and directly to those disciples who sat before him in the Luke Beatitudes ("Blessed are you when…"). Both occasions took place following an extensive healing ministry after which Jesus moved to a different location nearby to address his disciples. The Beatitudes were clearly for those who were, or wanted to be, his disciples.

There are other statements in the Gospels that begin with Jesus saying, "Blessed are…" I think they are also worthy of our consideration, and I have included them in these weeks of daily meditations. I have also included as the first beatitude the announcement of the blessedness of our Lord Jesus, who is the source, substance, and cause behind all other beatitudes. These inclusions bring the list of Beatitudes to the end of July and the conclusion of this book of meditations.

Please work and pray through these Beatitudes with your heart and mind, and with the gifts of Jesus' example, the Holy Spirit's guidance, and the assurance of the Father's love.

JULY 13

JESUS

Scripture for Reflection: Mathew 21:1-11

"Hosanna to the Son of David! Blessed is the one who comes in the name of the Lord!" (Matthew 21:9b, NRSV). These words were shouted by the crowd surrounding Jesus as he entered Jerusalem with no military escort and riding on a borrowed donkey. The crowd certainly did not begin to understand the full nature and extent of Jesus' mission. Most probably, many framed it as their liberation from the hated Roman government: "Surely, he's going to run out these pagan foreigners and restore our own independent Jewish nation. He will be our liberator! Let's pave the way by making a royal path with our own clothing and announcing his entrance by waving the palm branches of royalty! Yes, *Blessed is he!*"

It would not be unusual for people to call someone blessed who does them the great favor of advancing their own earthly interests. But that is not who Jesus calls blessed. He names as blessed those who are poor in spirit, grieving, meek, hungry, thirsty, persecuted for righteousness, merciful, pure of heart, peacemakers, those who are harassed for their righteousness and loyalty to God, the lied about, the faithful, the visionaries, the faithful servants, and the blessed of the Father. He is painting a picture of himself. The Beatitudes together are *a profile of Jesus*.

This blessedness of Jesus begins with the blessedness of God. Peter expresses the blessing in this way: "Blessed be the God and Father of our Lord Jesus Christ! By his great mercy he has given us new birth into a living hope through the resurrection of Jesus Christ from the dead…" (1 Peter 1:3, NRSV). Timothy speaks of "the glorious gospel of the blessed God that has been trusted to [him]" (1 Timothy 1:11b). Our blessed God, the origin and source of all blessedness, gives us his Son, incarnate in the human flesh of Jesus, who embodies the Beatitudes for us. The Beatitudes describe his life, his example, his experiences, his every expression of God's image, his holiness.

There was a *poverty* about Jesus. "Foxes have dens, and the birds in the sky have nests, but the Son of Man has no place to lay his head" (Matthew 8:20; Luke 9:58).

Jesus knew *grief*. He grieved when the religious authorities were more interested in keeping a Sabbath law than in rejoicing over the healing of someone's withered hand (Mark 3:1-5). He grieved over the death of Lazarus (John 11:35). He grieved over Jerusalem (Luke 19:41-44).

Jesus told his disciples that he was *gentle and humble* and ready to give them an easy yoke and a light burden (Matthew 11:29). Paul testified that Christ humbled himself to the point of death by crucifixion, a humbling for which God exalted him as Lord (Philippians 2:8-11).

Paul also testified that many are made righteous by the righteous act of the one who was himself *righteousness* in person—Jesus Christ our Lord (Romans 5:18-21).

The Gospels are replete with cries for *mercy*, to which Jesus never failed to respond (e.g., Matthew 15:22). His *heart purity*, tested by doubters, remained un-adulterated. His mission was one of *peace* (Luke 1:79c), and before his departure he bequeathed it to his disciples (John 14:27). A man *persecuted* beyond human endurance for his extraordinary righteousness, his wounds remain in our memory as the cost of our salvation and as encouragement when we negotiate the trials and sufferings of our witness as his followers.

Yes, the place to begin our consideration of the Beatitudes is to consider Jesus.

Dear Christ of the human road, I thank you for the blessing of your Beatitudes; and I especially thank you that your days on earth were living portraits of them all. As I meditate on them over these two weeks, stir my heart more to discover the depths of the life you lived and the lives you blessed. I pray this in your name, who gives us all the blessings worth having. Amen.

JULY 14

THE POOR IN SPIRIT AND THE POOR

Scripture for Reflection: Matthew 5:3; Luke 6:20b; James 2:5-7

In the first beatitude, Matthew records Jesus blessing "the poor in spirit," and Luke records Jesus blessing "you who are poor." In both settings, Jesus is addressing his disciples, those who were becoming his inner circle, and probably some others who were in the process of signing on. In Matthew's Gospel, Jesus is speaking broadly of all who are poor in spirit. In Luke's, he is specifically addressing poor people along with people who are about to become poor by virtue of becoming his disciples. We could conjecture that in Luke's Gospel, Jesus has the poor in spirit in mind when he says, "you poor," but I think it is more likely that on this occasion he, the impoverished Rabbi-Savior, is blessing his disciples in their accepting the inevitable poverty of giving him everything.

Sometimes acquiring possessions and assets has little to do with the possessions and assets themselves. Instead, those acquisitions have everything to do with the divine purpose for which they are entrusted to us and whether or not we are using them for a higher purpose. The question is not how much wealth we have; it is how we have our wealth, the purposes for which we put it in use, the ways we are or aren't distancing ourselves from it, and the safeguards we follow to keep it from consuming our lives and defining our security. Time and again, Jesus warns of the dangers of wealth. We, all of us who call ourselves disciples of Jesus, are asked to put our wealth, whether small or great, at the feet of Jesus, to make ourselves poor in spirit and not defined by our fiscal and material assets. To be sure, doing so is a far greater challenge for a materially wealthy follower of Jesus because the more the wealth, it seems, the more the desire for *more* wealth. Wealth easily becomes an addiction. But those without large assets can also become obsessively envious of and jealously preoccupied by the wealth others have—a kind of secondary addiction, if you like.

This brings us to the question of what Jesus meant by "the poor in spirit" in Mathew's passage. It's interesting that the Hebrew word for "poor" had come to carry the sense of "saintly" or "pious" in late Judaism, and it could be that this is the Aramaic word Jesus used here, translated by the Greek word for poor (*The Interpreter's Bible*, vol. 8, p.118). As there was this late association of poverty with holiness in Jewish thought, so there was a similar association in early Christianity. We see it in Paul's testimony of having come to the place of regarding everything as loss because of Christ (Philippians 3:7-9). Life in Christ is a journey, and you can't take much on a journey. You leave your gains behind so that you can travel with Christ. As with Paul, you count all your prospects, positions, and accomplishments as rubbish. You let this self-emptying mind be in you as it was in Christ Jesus.

The promise of life as a disciple of Jesus is made to those who have nothing save in Jesus—and know it. I remember a presentation by theologian Leonard Sweet years ago, which he closed with his own testimony in a way that was deeply moving. We saw projected on a large screen a sequence of paintings of Jesus as we listened to a recording of Fernando Ortega singing, "In the morning when I rise, give me Jesus. And when I am alone, give me Jesus. And when I come to die, you can have all this world, but give me Jesus." It's not that we're left without other blessings; it's that with Jesus comes everything that is *worth* having (1 Corinthians 3:21b-23).

Blessed are the poor in spirit; their poverty is filled with Jesus, his family of followers, and everything of eternal value. Blessed also are the poor who live with meager resources; God sees them and calls his poor-in-spirit disciples to support them, share love and resources with them, and help them to see how close they are to God's kingdom (James 2:5).

Do you have the blessing of spiritual poverty, and if not, are you ready to join?

Dear Jesus, thank you for impoverishing yourself for us and lavishly sharing with us the wealth that is eternal and the love that is transformative. Please forgive me if I put my status, position, and pursuit of things above your calling. Help me to detach myself from such worldly trivia and to attach myself to you—impoverished, self-giving, and motivated by your kind of love. I ask in your name, the name below and above all names. Amen.

JULY 15
THOSE WHO MOURN AND WEEP
Scripture for Reflection: Matthew 5:4; Luke 6:21b

Once again, the related beatitudes in Matthew and Luke's Gospels are worded differently. In Matthew's, Jesus blesses "those who mourn"; in Luke's, "you who weep now." The mourners "will be made glad"; the weepers "will laugh."

Let's begin with Luke's version, addressed to those who weep. As far as we know, only humans cry. Animals seem to have feelings of some kind, which they express in various ways, but they don't cry. We do.

"However they arrive," says Peter M. Marty, "tears remain a biological gift from God. They put us in touch with essential things that we know to be dear or wrong. And those things have a way of taking up residence in our hearts, often drawing us inadvertently closer to God. Giving ourselves permission to cry is valuable, especially if we want to trust the psalmist that sowing in tears can reap shouts of joy" (*Christian Century*, 4/20/22, p. 3).

It is certainly true that our crying can reveal holy motives. The two reports of Jesus weeping in the Gospels give us good clues. Holy weeping is weeping over someone else's loss or pain (Jesus weeping for Mary who is grieving over the death of her brother);

it is also weeping over the lostness of another (Jesus weeping over the people of Jerusalem who don't know what makes for peace). There is also deep and genuine weeping for joy in the midst of our own pain. Many can still recall the moving newsreels of Lou Gehrig in his departure speech at Yankee Stadium, forced into retirement by a disabling disease that came to be named after him, tearing up as he said to the crowd, "I'm the luckiest man on the face of the earth." Ironically, suffering does not block gratitude when we realize how deeply fortunate God has made our lives.

People cry over any number of other things: not getting their way, losing a game, being outdone by someone else, being treated unfairly—and the list of self-centered tears goes on and on. Holy weeping can begin only when we confess that our lives are self-centered and sinful, and we cry our way into repentance and forgiveness. Then, when God begins to free us of our selfish life, we can rejoice over this undeserved grace, weep over those who suffer, and laugh the strange laugh of those who own nothing and have everything. "All things are yours," says Paul, "and you belong to Christ, and Christ belongs to God" (1 Corinthians 3:21b, 23, NRSV).

The beatitude in Matthew 5:4 is a blessing of those who mourn or grieve. Jesus is obviously referring to those who are mourning for good reason—whether over the death of someone loved and treasured, over one's own sins leading to repentance and forgiveness, over the lostness of others, or over those who will suffer persecution as Jesus' disciples. Jesus is saying that on the other side of such sanctified or sanctifying mourning is consolation, a comforting, even a cheering up (all possible translations of the Greek word). In Luke's version of this beatitude, the corresponding condemnation is of those whose lives are merely the pursuit of laughter or self-indulgence. They will ultimately become mourners and weepers (Luke 6:25b). Divine reversals are common in so many of Jesus' teachings about the kingdom of God!

One of the mistakes some Christians make is thinking they must always be happy, show no sadness, ignore ugly realities, live in positive-thinking denial of dysfunction, conceal their struggles or sins. Living in such a fantasy world removes a person's capacity to mourn what needs mourning and affirm what really needs affirming. In a world suffused and corrupted by sin, robbed by death, and overrun with shallow self-seeking, Christ needs mourners. Not disciples who always look on the dark side and who you don't really want to be around, but disciples who mourn over what God mourns over and rejoice over what God rejoices over.

Dear Jesus, help me to mourn over what grieves your heart and rejoice over what brings you pleasure. And please convict me of pretense either way. I ask in your name. Amen.

JULY 16

THE HUMBLE

Scripture for Reflection: Matthew 5:5

In the past, most English versions of the New Testament translated the Greek word used in this verse as "the meek." Since then, that word has gradually been stripped of its beauty and is more typically used to describe someone without spine, a weakling. I remember a cartoon a few years ago with the words: "The meek will inherit the earth. They're too weak to refuse." So, the translation of the Greek that better captures Jesus' meaning today is "the humble" or "the humble-minded." The humility Jesus is talking about here is neither meek nor weak. We find it in those whose hearts are strong and whose lives don't need or seek the props of popularity, position, or power. They are the uncompromised, content with next to nothing, trustworthy with everything.

The key to it, says the apostle Paul, is our relationship with Christ. Speaking personally, Paul describes that relationship this way:

> "I consider everything a loss in comparison with the superior value of knowing Christ Jesus my Lord. I have lost everything for him, but what I lost I think of as sewer trash, so that I might gain Christ and be found in him. In Christ I have a righteousness that is not my

own and that does not come from the Law but rather from the faithfulness of Christ" (Philippians 3:8-9a).

Originally, Paul's special claim to righteousness came through his mastery of the Jewish Law and through his persecution of non-conforming Jews. When Christ confronts him and blinds him so that he can see in a different way, he realizes that his current righteousness is not what he thought. It now appears as "sewer trash." That's quite humbling! Without a righteousness that is not his own, he feels lost. The humble teenager, Mary, who became the mother of Jesus, prophesied years before that this Jesus in her womb would pull down the powerful and lift the lowly (Luke 1:52). In fact, says Jesus later, those lowly ones will "inherit the earth."

Let this self-emptying mind be in you that was in Christ Jesus, says a Paul now stripped of his assets (Philippians 2:5). The promise of life in Christ is made to those who now know they have nothing of their own worth keeping, so they give it back. Everything. Having been saved in our poverty, we see ourselves as belonging to Christ. That includes all our assets, as well.

This is what it means to find our true selves. When we are able to see ourselves devoid of this world's measurements of success and humbled in the presence of Christ, we are seeing into our souls, our God-given identity. There is no virtue, per se, in having nothing. And there is certainly a kind of false righteousness that comes in claiming spiritual superiority because we have rejected the benefits that God has allowed to come our way. Nor is it a measure of our holiness not to accept accountability for how we use the gifts God has given us. But, however many our assets, we will never know joy unless we know the emptiness that Christ fills with his undeserved grace. "The only ones who come up full," says John Fischer, "are the ones who are willing to be presented empty" (*Real Christians Dance*, Bethany House Publishers, 1988, p. 53).

Lyell Rader reminded me of the humble whom Christ blessed. A well-educated man—in fact a true scholar—he let neither his keen insights nor his brilliant, eloquent writing be a cause of pride. He published only occasional articles, never a book. He preferred deferring to others in group discussions. When he was asked to be a speaker at a conference, listeners were impressed both by the depth of what he said and by his unassuming manner. It was a profile in humility. He and his wife Elaine, Salvation Army officers, retired quietly to a simple life together. He passed away a few years ago, leaving the inheritance of earth to other humble followers of Christ.

For me, Lyell is a model of the humility I seek. Do you have the model you need?

Dear Jesus, sanctify my heart and mold me to your humble likeness. I pray in your name. Amen.

JULY 17

Those Who Are Hungry and Thirsty for Righteousness

Scripture for Reflection: Matthew 5:6; Luke 6:21

Here, again, we come across a seeming difference between the persons being addressed in this beatitude—in this case, what they are hungering for. In Matthew's Gospel, Jesus is speaking in general to those who are hungry and thirsty for righteousness; and in Luke's Gospel, with the absence of the word "righteousness" and with the use of "you who hunger," Jesus seems to be addressing specific people in the crowd who are simply hungry. The other difference is Luke not including "thirsting."

The word "righteousness" has a long history in Scripture and a meaning that is often misunderstood. It is not a thing or a condition that we can acquire and permanently possess, as if we could then say we have it for life. It is something that happens in a particular relationship. Think of all our relationships: with parents, siblings, spouse, our children, our grandchildren, our friends, our neighbors, our fellow church members, other races and ethnicities, competitors, even those who consider themselves to be our enemies—and the list goes on and includes the whole world that God loves and gave his life for (John 3:16). The Creator has placed us in these relationships for specific purposes in accord with his will. Righteousness in any one of them is to fulfill the divine purpose of that relationship.

God, of course, is the wholly Righteous One who, as the Creator of everything and everyone, has always acted righteously in his relationship to all his creation and has called us to do the same in all our relationships. We are the ones, however, to whom he has also given the freedom to do otherwise—that is, to choose to be or not to be righteous in our relationships. For example, many Christians over the years have acted (and still do) unrighteously toward Jews. Christians who have worked hard and taken risks to fight anti-Semitism and protect the lives and rights of Jews are often designated by our Jewish brothers and sister as 'righteous Gentiles.'

Our dilemma is that we may act righteously in one relationship by fulfilling God's intention for that relationship, but not in another. We may act righteously toward a friend but not toward a spouse, or vice versa. We may even act righteously toward others and not toward ourselves. Our righteousness may be selective. Or we may heavily invest in our relationship with God while failing to invest ourselves in our relationship with our own children. How can this happen? It can happen when we approach our relationship with God as one-dimensional, a closed, exclusive relationship that may make us feel spiritual in a *cozy* way, but which goes contrary to the spiritual expansiveness for which he created us. The claim that we have been sanctified and given a pure heart by God is meaningless if we are not intentionally investing ourselves in how we can live and embody that blessing *in all our relationships.*

The beatitude blesses those who are "hungry and thirsty for righteousness." Hunger and thirst are experiences that must repeat themselves or we die. They express a longing for sustenance needed for survival and prosperity. We hunger for God's reviving and restoring presence, so we seek his face in solitude and prayer. We hunger for the love and support of fellow Christians, so we engage with them for our shared growth in grace and discipleship. The God who, in Jesus, fed the poor is deeply concerned about those who cannot get the food they need, so he calls us to the righteousness of feeding the hungry, a calling to which many Christians give themselves fully—but there are not enough of them. He calls us to the righteousness of opposing specific forms of abuse and discrimination, a calling that was taken seriously by Charles G. Finney, the famous American evangelist who in 1835 agreed to be a professor at Oberlin College only on the condition that the college observe no color line. It takes the forms of investing more fully in our friendships, or our marriage, or our relations at work, or ____. You can fill in the blank for yourself. Be at peace. Righteousness is a lifelong journey of improvement and growth for us all.

Righteous God, thank you that my hunger for righteousness will be filled. Help me at this moment to hear and obey your call to begin living out your righteousness in the particular relationship to which I now hear you calling me. I pray this through Jesus. Amen.

JULY 18

Those Who Show Mercy

Scripture for Reflection: Matthew 5:7; Luke 10:30-37

Mercy is a quality we ascribe to God because we know he is willing to give us far better than we deserve. He is gracious and forgiving. He grants us more grace than is fair. Where we are quick to say about some, "They got what they deserved," God is quick to go beyond justice. In fact, he might just wipe a person's slate of guilt clean. We call that mercy.

Think of a court of law where the defendant is convicted of a crime based on sufficient evidence and then goes to prison. That is fairness. Think of a court of law where the defendant admits his guilt and the judge, convinced of the defendant's sincere sorrow, sets the man free under certain conditions. That is mercy. God is indeed a fair God; he affirms us for the good we do. God is also a merciful God. His compassion is not throttled by our sin; it is multiplied to the extent of the grace needed by those who sincerely confess their sins and start over.

Jesus, of course, is our model and giver of mercy. Lest we are under the illusion that some of us don't really need mercy, we should pay attention to this beatitude. Jesus says that the merciful are the ones who will "receive mercy." If the merciful need mercy themselves, then *we all need it!* To think we don't is to live under the illusion that all our thoughts, motivations, and actions are holy, pure, and love-based—which is only true of Jesus, merciful God in human flesh. On the other hand, it is not true that some of us are incapable of being merciful. If so, it would be cruel for Jesus to say in his description of the Final Judgment that only those who were merciful toward the starving, those clothed in rags, and the imprisoned would inherit God's kingdom (Matthew 25:31-46). The capacity for mercy resides in us all.

How, then, is it to be found and released, especially in we who are beginners in mercy? In the story of the Final Judgment, we have a good clue. First of all, Jesus says that those who will inherit God's kingdom are those who fed and clothed him and visited him in prison. None of them to whom he says this have any memory of doing that to Jesus. Jesus explains it in one of the most startlingly beautiful mysteries of God's incarnation: "I assure you that when you have done it for one of the least of these brothers and sisters of mine, you have done it for me" (v. 40).

Mother Teresa, who ministered to the poor of Calcutta, had a prayer that she called "Jesus My Patient." It went like this:

> Dearest Lord, may I see you today and every day in the person of your sick, and, while nursing them, minister to you.... Though you hide yourself behind the unattractive disguise of the irritable, the exacting, the unreasonable, may I still recognize you, and say: "Jesus, my patient, how sweet it is to serve you." ("Jesus my Patient," quoted by Malcolm Muggeridge in *Something Beautiful for God: Mother Teresa of Calcutta* [New York: Harper and Row, 1971], pp. 74-75)

I suspect that because of Jesus' Final Judgment story, some of us may wonder if we qualify for heaven since we are not involved in ministries to the poor, the sick, and the imprisoned. We need to remember, however, that there are disciples of Jesus who have a special gift and heart for this mission. The Scriptures are clear, however, that the poor and outcast are of particular concern to God and that he expects us all to participate with our help in whatever ways we can. Who knows? We may find that our gifts and skills are exactly what a marginalized person needs!

God's mercy lives in us because we are the reclamations of that mercy. As imperfectly as we may be carriers of it, we have been transformed by it. And in one way or another, we must let that transformation show in the way we share compassion with those who don't deserve it, as Christ has shared more compassion with us than we could ever deserve.

Time and again, people approached Jesus because they saw mercy in him. "Jesus, have mercy on me" was a common plea (e.g., Matthew 15:22). Hopefully, they also see something of the same mercy in you and me. And just maybe, the Christ in us will make us enough like him that we will become conduits of the divine mercy they desperately need.

Merciful God, thank you for revealing and releasing your mercy in the person of Jesus, our Savior and Lord. Through your Spirit, please empower me to show mercy, especially to those who don't deserve it, just as I don't. In the name of our merciful Jesus. Amen.

JULY 19
THOSE WHO HAVE PURE HEARTS
Scripture for Reflection: Matthew 5:8

We must begin this meditation by answering two questions: what did Jesus mean by "pure" and what did he mean by "heart"? The Jews practiced ritual purification and forbade the eating of food considered unclean. Jesus was more focused on moral purity and said that nothing going into us was defiling, only what came out in our words and actions (Mark 7:15). Purity is a singleness of motive, the opposite of the "doublemindedness" of those who are "unstable in all their ways" (James 1:5-8). The unpurified may have some good qualities but their intentions are mixed.

In Jesus' day, the word "heart" was used to designate a person's inner self and included what we would call in combination our emotions, our mind, and our will. A person's heart is pure when there is harmony between all three—or to say it differently, when all three work together to express God's love and to realize his purpose for our lives. How can this happen? Our emotions are unstable and often unpredictable. Our minds are limited and often confused. And our will is sometimes, or often, weak and divided. So, where do we start?

If we were to focus on what satisfies our emotions, our lives would be an emotional rollercoaster and the strength of our faith would depend on emotional highs. If, on the other hand, we were to focus on the beliefs and doctrines we embrace, dry concepts would begin to replace faith in a living God. And yet, our emotions are an important part of our faith experience, and there is no such thing as a mindless Christianity. But it is the will that seems to be the key. Christianity is a life to be lived, and this life is possible only to the extent that we allow God to inhabit and guide our will. The paradox of this inhabitation by God is not that he then controls our will; rather, he gives back to us the will that has been seduced and corrupted by a fallen world. Apart from God, we are not ourselves—our true selves. "My will is not my own/ till thou hast made it thine," says a line from the George Matheson hymn, "I Have No Claim on Grace."

Perhaps the best way to see our Christian journey is to see it as walking Christ's way of life, guided by the Spirit, motivated by God's love. John Wesley struggled to find such a walk, and it was not until he came to a meeting in Aldersgate after returning from his failed ministry in America, that he found his heart "strangely warmed." This experience began to work itself out in his life as a purifying of his heart, a growing alignment of his will with God's will, his emotions with God's love, and his thinking with the mind of God. "Purity of heart," said Kierkegaard, "is to will one thing." And that "one thing" is what God wills for our lives.

The greatest commandment, says Jesus, is this: "You must love the Lord your God with all your heart, with all your being, and with all your mind." And the next to the greatest commandment is like it: "You must love your neighbor as you love yourself" (Matthew 22:37-39). The "must love" is important. Loving God and loving our neighbors is a 'must' choice for those seeking purity of heart because loving God and loving our neighbors *is* heart purity. John Wesley's brother Charles was the hymn-writer whose eloquent hymns were as insightful, if not more so, than John's theology. Here is a verse from his hymn "O for a Heart to Praise My God":

> A heart in every thought renewed
> And full of love divine,
> Perfect and right and pure and good,
> A copy, Lord, of thine.

This in no way means that our love for God and others will always be amply expressed or a credible expression of Christ's love. In moments of unsteady emotions and/or confused thinking, our actions may not reflect purity of heart, the one thing to be willed. God's gift to us in such times is forgiving grace and the humility to confess our sins to and with one another. And as our hearts are being strengthened and purified, our vision of God will become clearer, until the day when we see him as he is.

God of love, purify my heart more and more so that I will be more like Christ. When I fail, please tell me. When I am confused, please give me clarity. When I am too confident, humble me. I ask in the name of Jesus, the pure heart. Amen.

JULY 20

THE PEACEMAKERS

Scripture for Reflection: Matthew 5:9; Ephesians 2:14-16

Peacemaking is one of the most frustrating enterprises on the planet, even among Christians. So many are not at peace with themselves, their families, their church, their neighborhood community, or their world. They get depressed, have family fights, quit their church, isolate themselves from their neighborhood, or remain in despair about the prospects of world peace. Christians claim to follow the Prince of Peace, whose birth was announced by angels as the coming of "peace on earth" (Luke 2:14), and whose last words to his disciples were "My peace I give you. My peace I leave with you" (John 14:27a). And yet so many of his followers today can't seem to make peace even with each other. The Christian population often divides itself into camps that dismiss other camps of Christians. Jesus' prayer to the Father that his disciples would be one, just as he and the Father were one (John 17:21), seems a long way off.

The beatitude we are considering is not a beatitude about peace itself; it is a beatitude about peace*making*. Peace is not an automatic; it must be made—and Jesus did not say it would be easy. It cost him his life to bring peace to earth, and it will cost us to dare to be his peacemakers. There are two ways we are tempted to avoid our calling to be peacemakers. One is to convince ourselves that real peace is unattainable in this fallen world and possible only in the future transformed world we call heaven. Another is a spiritualized version of peace where we claim and protect only a peace *within*, a peace we covet for ourselves—a selfish, private peace. Both dismiss the call of Jesus to be his peacemakers.

Jesus put his peacemaking on the line. With his own body, he broke down the barrier of hatred dividing us. On the cross, he made one new group out of two unreconciled groups, one body out of two (Ephesians 2:14-16). He is still doing it where his disciples are accepting their call to be peacemakers. Seeking to be reconcilers in this world where people don't trust those who are different or think differently can be risky. It calls people out of their walled-in tribal comfort zones; and, feeling threatened, they resist. Built-in prejudices toward "different" groups send the message that peace is impossible. Jesus says that it *is* possible and that our cowardice in not actively pursuing it is our failure to believe in his mission to bring peace on earth.

Some will point out that Jesus once said he had come to bring not peace but a sword and that his ministry would have the result of turning family members against each other (Matthew 10:34-36). Obviously, that was not Jesus' intent, but he recognized that it would often be the result where some family members were threatened by another member's conversion to a pacifist Christ and the radical lifestyle of his disciples. The life of someone living in the peace of Christ is a judgment on those whose lives are grounded on the premises of hatred and exclusion.

Christ gave everything to gift us with a peace that has spiritual power, the power to risk crossing lines and sharing Christlike love with strangers and enemies. Dag Hammarskjold,

RENEWALS

a worldwide peacemaker, did it through his service as Secretary General of the United Nations. A devout Christian who kept a spiritual diary and worked tirelessly for world peace, he didn't let the failures to bring peace in some situations diminish the successes in others.

But not all of us can be peacemakers on the international level. No less important, and in some ways more important, is peacemaking at a local level. The name that comes immediately to my mind is David Laeger, a Salvation Army officer. A very quiet man, his silences were not withdrawals and escapes, they were listenings, a deeper involvement with what was at hand, the living out of a deeper peace that made his presence want us not to take sides but rather to listen to God. If you were to read his poetry, you would find the peace of Christ in the words.

In what way does God want you to use your uniqueness to be his peacemaker?

Peacemaker Christ, I ask you to rid me of my divisiveness and to instill in me a deep commitment to the ministry of reconciliation. In your name I pray. Amen.

July 21

Those Who Are Persecuted for Their Righteousness

Scripture for Reflection: Matthew 5:10; 1 Peter 1:6-9

People suffer persecution for different reasons. Usually, the persecution is carried out by people who hold power or represent a majority that give overt or tacit support to the persecutors. Racial, ethnic, and impoverished minorities are frequently persecuted by majorities. Established political parties sometimes use their power to demean or persecute newer parties or political movements. Religious minorities are frequent targets of those whose religion—usually more established (and often more compromised)—is threatened by a new and more vibrant expression of that same religion or by a different religion that appears at first to be a threat.

Followers of the crucified and resurrected Jesus began to evangelize and train new disciples. They spread across the Mediterranean world, and people started taking notice. Increasing numbers were won over by the gospel preached and the new life in Christ offered. As the movement continued to spread, people noticed that these Christians lived by a new holiness. The radical love of Jesus called Christians to apply this love to every relationship in their lives. As imperfectly as they may have lived by this creed, their way of life was still revolutionary.

It shook people out of their complacency, precipitating either conversions or oppositions. The opposers were those who were not prepared to pay the price for such a love-based life. It would have required a change so radical as to undermine the premises on which their lives had been built.

The persecutions of Christians came slowly and sporadically but come they did. The irony is that the persecutions did not stop the growth of the Christian movement; it even seemed to fuel it! Why was that? The answer in a single word is *righteousness*. The kingdom of heaven, said Jesus, belongs to those who endure suffering for their righteousness.

In an earlier meditation (July 17), we saw Jesus blessing those who were "hungry and thirsty for righteousness." Here, we see him blessing those who are persecuted for *being* righteous, paying a steep price for loving and giving ultimate allegiance to Christ and not Caesar; loving their neighbors as much as they love themselves; loving even those who turn against them because they are threatened (or judged) by this extraordinary righteousness. The persecutions enhance the righteousness, shame the persecutors, and win new converts. It also culls Christians who are not at the time ready to pay the price of this radical righteousness. Later, some Christians who remain faithful oppose allowing the "deserters" back into the fellowship following the periods of persecution. Heroes can be prideful of their heroism, robbing it of a righteous motive. Other Christian survivors of persecution are more gracious, welcoming the repentant back into a forgiving fold, now ready to pay the price.

The apostle Peter wrote a passage in his first letter to the Gentile Christians in Asia Minor who were beginning to suffer persecution for their Christian faith. He said that these trials would serve to make their faith genuine, pure as gold. Let us not confuse this with the mental illness called masochism: seeking pleasure and sometimes attention from being dominated, hurt, or persecuted by someone. This is a serious mental sickness calling for spiritual and psychological healing. Those who suffer for the sake of righteousness are not begging for attention; they are only seeking to live the life of Jesus in a world that may take exception and respond hatefully.

I am sure everyone reading this meditation has at some time or another failed the test of righteousness, as I have, when the cost seemed too much. You may confess this, maybe with a brother or sister in Christ, receive forgiveness, and be strengthened for the next opportunity.

Dear Jesus, Righteousness in Person, thank you for paying full price for our freedom from sin and through your Spirit, empowering us for the courage of divine love in all our relationships. Please give me the measure of courage I need to reflect your love and embody your righteousness when I feel threatened. I pray this in your name. Amen.

JULY 22

THE INSULTED AND MALIGNED

Scripture for Reflection: Matthew 5:11-12; Luke 6:22-23

There is a suffering for Christ's sake that seems milder than the persecution we described in the last meditation. It is more subtle and undercover. It expresses itself in harassments, insults, stereotypes, hatred, exclusion, and jokes. Opposition to Christians has largely gone underground since Christianity is still the largest religion in most Western nations. It has been replaced by opposition of Christians to other Christians and to other religions.

Whereas some scholars consider Matthew 5:10-12 as one beatitude, it seems to me that verse 10 (considered in the previous meditation) is specifically focused on a more strident, life-threatening persecution, and verses 11 and 12 on more indirect forms of belittlement and humiliation, even shaming. Furthermore, Luke's fourth beatitude (Luke 6:22-23) seems more aligned with Matthew 5:11-12. It speaks of the hatreds, insults, and condemnations Christians endure.

The early Christians were not treated brutally as often as they were harassed, insulted, made fun of, and discriminated against. Their beliefs—the resurrection, for example—were hard to understand. Their practices—the love feast, for example—seemed suspicious. Their ethics—loving their enemies, for example—seemed totally unrealistic. Christians were downright strange and were usually treated as such; and the shunning was sometimes hard to take.

In our secularized age, most people seem to prefer keeping their religion, if they have one at all, as a private matter. Everyone has a right to their own beliefs, and no one has the right to impose theirs on someone else. I attended a very secular university in the late 50s and early 60s. Religious conversations and discussions of one's faith were uncommon and usually took place between those who knew each other well and shared the same faith. The Bible and religion courses were taught as a part of history. I remember one student who made a point of trying to befriend fellow students to use it as an opportunity to share the gospel. He never seemed to succeed. He was shunned and made the butt of jokes. But he soldiered on, while I, for the most part, kept quiet about my Christian faith, unless asked.

Keitha told me about a young Salvationist who was drafted in the military and used to kneel by his bed and pray in the barracks before going to bed. His fellow soldiers called him GI Jesus. I'm sure Charlie Olsen knew that for some, the name meant respect and for others, derision. I'm confident that he did not try to push his faith on others, but he let his life be the witness. I'm also confident he was open to praying with any who were seeking God.

In a world of both the religiously disinterested and those of other faiths, it is the living out of our faith that will draw some to Christ and scare others away. Christians whose lives embody the radical love of Jesus will attract those seeking a life of deeper relationships and meaning, and they will repel those who cling desperately to the rewards of self-advancement and materialism. Some who are repelled may claim the identity of Christians, but their faith is rendered impotent by their obsessive pursuit of their own pleasure and success.

There has been an interesting shift in the pattern of maligning other faith practices. It began centuries ago and continues to this day. It is one Christian group (denomination) openly labeling and attacking another one as heretical, disobedient, compromised, or too lax. The early church, however, did not base its Christian legitimacy on attacking other religions or other Christians. Its focus was the gospel mission and the making of disciples. Perhaps we could learn from them and quit attacking Jews, Muslims, and other Christian groups. It only undermines our legitimacy as followers of the Prince of Peace.

Jesus, please help me to see the goodness and love in other Christians and non-Christians that practice their faith differently from the ways I practice mine. Help me to see others through your eyes and not my prejudiced, judgmental mind. I ask in your name. Amen.

JULY 23

Those Who Are Not Scandalized by the Crucified Jesus

Scripture for Reflection: Matthew 11:6; Luke 7:23

John the Baptist wants a definitive answer from Jesus: "Are you the one who is to come, or should we look for another?" (Mathew 11:2-3; Luke 7:18-19). We can speculate about John's state of mind. Does he simply want more assurance that Jesus is the long-awaited Messiah? Is he disappointed that the new messianic kingdom does not seem to have arrived as he had expected? Jesus certainly hasn't got the majestic trappings of the conquering messiah of popular belief. Is John beginning to doubt or perhaps wonder? At the least, he wants some assurance. There are rumors that both religious leaders and Roman government officials are plotting to do away with this self-proclaimed messianic figure. Is it all about to come to an end with Jesus' death?

You will remember that no one else that we know of realized that Jesus' death by crucifixion was to be the fulfillment, not the end, of his saving mission. When Jesus had predicted that he would be killed and raised on the third day, Peter said, "Forbid, Lord! This won't happen to you" (Matthew 16:21-22). His disciples, thinking it was all over when he was arrested, were to forsake him and flee (Mark 14:50). On the third day after the crucifixion, two disciples traveling to Emmaus were joined by

— 179 —

the now resurrected Jesus, whom they did not recognize at first. Jesus told them that the Messiah's suffering and death were foreseen by the prophets as the necessary gateway to salvation and new life, and when he broke bread with them, they recognized him (Luke 24:13-32) and they soon confirmed his resurrection with the other disciples (vv. 33-35).

The stumbling block of the gospel was now revealed: a faith centered on a crucified man whom God resurrected. Salvation through a cross of execution, eternal life through a resurrection from the dead. The Jesus who humbled himself to the point of death is exalted by the Father to universal Lordship (Philippians 2:7-11). Paul warns, don't be seduced by "clever words" that empty the cross of its meaning. "The message of the cross is foolishness to those who are being destroyed. But it is the power of God for those who are being saved" (1 Corinthians 1:18).

The cross is a scandal to a world that honors getting more and more, gaining power over others, looking good all the time, cleverly succeeding—a world that honors winners and wants no part of Jesus' invitation to take up our cross and follow him (Matthew 10:38; 16:24-27). But the cross, says the New Testament, is the very reason for our boasting. It is how the world has been crucified to us through Christ, and we have been crucified to the world (Galatians 6:14). It is also through the cross that a very diverse church is reconciled as one Body (Ephesians 2:16). In fact, says Colossians 1:20, Jesus' crucifixion was God's way of "reconciling all things to himself ... whether things on earth or in the heavens." This wide salvation sounded too threatening to the hometown synagogue in Nazareth when Jesus' sermon suggested that God's love had extended beyond their religious tribe. They attempted to throw him off a cliff (Luke 4:28-30).

Those Who Are Not Scandalized by the Crucified Jesus

The cross of Jesus stands as the center of our faith and as the source of our lives as disciples of Jesus. It graces us with what none of us deserves. It includes every race and ethnicity. It humbles the respectable and gives respect to the humble. It is the great leveler, making penitents of us all. That is the scandal of it, but a scandal only to those locked in pursuit of their own interests whatever the costs. A scandal—literally a stumbling block or something that causes us to stumble when we are lost in our own self-obsessed world.

Blessed are those who are not scandalized by the crucified Jesus.

Blessed Jesus, universal Savior who did not spare
yourself so that anyone can be saved, I sing my
praise to you with John Bowring's words:
In the cross of Christ I glory
Towering o'er the wrecks of time;
All the light of sacred story
Gathers round its head sublime.
Amen.

JULY 24

THOSE WITH EYES TO SEE AND EARS TO HEAR

Scripture for Reflection: Matthew 13:16-17; Luke 10:23-24

It's a curious thing that two people can look at the same thing and not see the same thing, or listen to the same thing and not hear the same thing. It depends on what we're looking or listening for—what we're conditioned to look for, or what we're conditioned to hear. One looks at a certain work of art and sees something that reaches at a deep level; another looks at it, and there is no such penetration, only puzzlement. Seeing and hearing is not simply a matter of the thing we're seeing or hearing: it reaches the view at a deeper level, what we are predisposed to see or hear, what we're looking for or listening for in the first place. This does not mean there is no such thing as something that is true in and of itself. It only means that the truth may affect us in different ways or that we may respond to it in different ways. We may decide either to believe it or not to believe it.

Our predisposition to see or hear in certain ways is a matter of both our personal inclinations and preferences, and the conditioning of our life experiences. More importantly, it's also a matter of our motivation. Helen Keller was born without the ability to see or hear, but she found ways to become a keen visionary and listener. Her motivation was cultivated by her stubborn, dedicated lifelong teacher and companion, Anne Sullivan, who taught Helen different ways to see and hear. Helen, in turn, taught the world.

Jesus also teaches us new ways to see and hear. He is asked by his disciples why he speaks in parables when he addresses the crowds. His answer is that though the crowds see, they don't *really* see; and though they hear, they don't really listen or understand. He calls this the fulfillment of a prophecy of Isaiah. And speaking directly to his disciples, he says, "Blessed are your eyes, for they see, and your ears for they hear" (Matthew 13:10-17, NRSV).

Jesus teaches us and gifts us with a different way to see and hear by using the eyes and ears of faith. Speaking of his later disciples who would not have known Jesus during his life on earth or witnessed his resurrection appearances, he says, "Blessed are those who have not seen and yet have come to believe" (John 20:29b, NRSV). There is a way to see beyond seeing and to hear beyond hearing. And it is available to all of us.

The eyes and ears of faith center on Jesus. Even before Jesus' birth, his mother Mary visits her cousin Elizabeth, who is herself pregnant with the future John the Baptist. Elizabeth, feeling unusual movement in her own womb, takes it as a sign from God: "Blessed is she [Mary] who believed that there would be a fulfillment of what was spoken to her by the Lord" (Luke 1:45). By appearance and the Messiah talk going around, this teenage working-class girl does not seem to be the best choice to bear the one called "God's Son" (v. 35c). But Mary and Elizabeth see and hear with the eyes and ears of faith.

The question Jesus poses for all of us is not so much, "What are you seeing and hearing?" Rather, it is "Who are you seeing and hearing?" The *who* comes before the *what*. The important

RENEWALS

thing is to see and hear Jesus. To do this, we familiarize ourselves with Scripture—the Gospels in particular. We spend time with Jesus in personal prayer and meditation. And we allow ourselves to be taught about Jesus by our church and by good Christian mentors. These put us in readiness to see the vision and hear the voice of our Lord.

So here are questions worth answering wherever we may be on our Christian journey:

- What part of Jesus' teachings in the Gospels am I working on personally?
- What is the best way I've discovered to spend time with Jesus daily, and am I doing it?
- In what ways am I getting support and wisdom from my church and my discipleship companions?

Prayer suggestion: Center your prayer on one of the questions above.

July 25

Those Who Are Faithful Servants

Scripture for Reflection: Luke 12:35-44

While Keitha and I (not yet married but thinking about it) were students at the University of Miami, Jim and Ruth Osborne came to be our corps officers (the ministers where we worshiped and served). They planned good worship services, and their preaching was always well prepared. They visited their church members consistently and were very attentive to the hospitalized. They used Sunday school to teach the faith and attract new participants; and they gave full support and provided resources to the teachers. We were among a group of college and high school students; the Osbornes met with us as a group and encouraged us to see our future as a calling. They were faithful stewards of the church while at the same time carrying responsibility for The Salvation Army's social services in huge Miami-Dade County!

Jim and Ruth were very gifted pastors and leaders, but I want to highlight their stewardship. To use the language of Jesus' two stories recorded In Luke 12:35-44, they were both good stewards who faithfully and diligently served their Lord (vv. 35-40) and good supervisors who treated their workers compassionately and fairly (vv. 41-44). In the first of those stories, Jesus commends the stewardship of all the servants in the household. No one is singled out, I imagine, because the supervisor nurtured a unity and cohesiveness by encouraging and working alongside the staff himself. Totally involving himself with them must have given the staff strong motivation to do their very best. The master, coming home from a late-night marriage celebration is overwhelmed and overjoyed by the readiness of all the staff to serve him and by the prime condition of his household. He (yes, he the *master*!) dresses himself for service and waits on and serves his servants. In the second story, the master commends the managers of a household because they give the servants their food at the proper time and help them to be diligent in fulfilling all their responsibilities. The reward here is that all the faithful managers will share in the stewardship of the master's wealth.

Both stories are about Jesus' return and the condition in which he finds his faith community. There are those who begin strong, but over time, take their eternal security for granted. They cease nurturing their spiritual life and become lax in their service. They drift into a dangerous negligence, forgetting that the time of Jesus' return will be as unpredictable as a thief in the night (v. 40). In telling this story, Jesus is not summoning his followers to live scared; he is calling them to live out their conversion by growing in grace. The Christian life is a journey ever toward Jesus and never to be taken for granted. Jesus says, "Be dressed for service"—literally, "Let your loins be girded"—meaning, get out of the long, impressive robe that holds you down and dress yourself for action! And keep the lamps of your stewardship lit so that you can see and address the challenges ahead (v. 35).

Perhaps the supreme beauty of the first story is the utter humility of the master of the house. When he returns and finds all his servants still awake, having done their duties and now eagerly awaiting the return of their master, he defies tradition and takes on the servant role. He removes his beautiful robe and girds himself with humility, serving those who are called to serve *him*. "I am among you as one who serves," says Jesus (22:27c). Of course.

If any of us complain about the lowliness of our calling, we should consider the lowliness of the real Master. Remember that we are those privileged to be served by Jesus, and we should know how important we are because of it. And whatever our status in the church hierarchy, in truth we are all mere servants, and we ought to act like it. And Jesus will bless us for it.

Thank you, Jim and Ruth, for showing us what that looks like.

Dear Servant Jesus, thank you for showing us what servanthood really is. Please keep sending people our way to show us how we can be better servants of you and each other. Help me to emulate your life and especially your humility. In your name I pray. Amen.

JULY 26

THE GIVERS

Scripture for Reflection: Acts 20:17-38

These verses describe the apostle Paul's farewell meeting with the church elders of Ephesus. He is on his way to Jerusalem, even though he has been warned that he would encounter threats to his life from the enemies of this new Christian movement. On the way, he is visiting some of the churches he founded, and now he is meeting with the elders of Ephesus. His ministry at Ephesus had extended over two years. He knows and loves this church, and they him.

In this final meeting, he recalls and describes his ministry over those two years. He is now instructing them by the example he set. He lived among them in humility and shared their trials and sorrows. He took no advantage of them, nor sought to profit from them. He taught them both publicly and in their homes. He evangelized both Greeks and Jews. He testified to the good news of God's grace. He shared the entire plan of God for them. He shepherded the young church. Now he challenges them to be good shepherds of their flock. He warns them of the threat of "wolves" who would try to destroy their flock and distort the Word to lure their own followers.

At this point he seems to depart from his admonitions about their spiritual leadership. He turns their attention from themselves and their responsibilities as spiritual leaders to the weaker people under their charge. He knows it is easy for them to get so caught up in the multiple leadership roles of their calling that they ignore the more vulnerable members of the community. So, he insists that the focus of their hard work must include helping the weak.

Paul then seems suddenly to recall words spoken by Jesus. (They do not occur in any of the four Gospels, but we know there were separate remembrances and collections of Jesus' teachings at the time.) This saying certainly reflects much of what Jesus taught and what his life exemplified. It is not at all difficult to hear our Lord say, "It is more blessed to give than to receive" (Acts 20: 35b). These are the last recorded words of Paul shared with the Ephesian elders. They all kneel to pray. Their final minutes together are filled with tears. They never see Paul again.

Receiving God's gifts is good because the nature of it is that the recipient becomes a giver. If the recipient does not become a giver, he has only become a taker. Jesus himself was a giver in whom dwelt all the fullness of God. He gave, and gave, and gave again, just like our heavenly Father whose generosity is without limit. As those who are created in God's image, our calling is to give of ourselves to others, especially the weak and the vulnerable. Those to whom we give ourselves, however, are not only those whose needs are apparent. They are all of us, who at one time or another are in some way weak or vulnerable and in need of a giver who can help. All true givers have also been gracious receivers of help, which is why they know better how to give and want to do so for others. Those who think they never need help themselves cannot be good givers.

Today, a follower of Jesus needs to recognize his own need

RENEWALS

for help and to look for a trusted giver. He knows where his vulnerabilities and weaknesses lie. We live in a world of takers, however, who deny their vulnerabilities by acquiring one thing after another to cover the pain of their spiritual starvation. Sadly, even some Christians are seduced by this culture of more and more, identifying their acquisitions and wealth with "God's blessing." Taking is not receiving because there is no grace in it, proven by the lack of giving to others what has been taken.

None of us are called to be takers. We are called to be gracious receivers of God's blessings so that we can be generous givers to those who are in need. And Jesus will bless us for it as he makes us more like him in our giving. It is more blessed to give than to receive because giving away is the fulfillment of all that we receive.

Dear Jesus, who received what was given by the Father and gave to us what he received, help me to receive your gifts with gratitude and share them graciously. Help me also to surrender my pride by humbly asking and receiving from others the helping grace I need, so that I can, in turn, be more and more a giver like you. In your name, amen.

July 27

The Open-Table Hosts

Scripture for Reflection: Luke 14:1-14

The passage above begins with the account of an out-of-place dinner guest. Jesus has been invited to a Sabbath meal at the home of a leader of the Pharisees. When he arrives, he notices a man suffering from an abnormal swelling of the body. Rabbinic tradition falsely associates this condition with a sexually transmitted disease. In the eyes of the Pharisees, that's reason enough to keep their distance. Jesus, of course, comes closer. This man's need supersedes tradition and discomfort. He knows it's the Sabbath and senses the religious professionals are anxious to accuse. With no hesitation, he heals the man anyway. "Wouldn't you immediately rescue your own child or your own ox who has fallen into a ditch even though it happens to be the Sabbath?" (Luke 14:5). Not waiting for the obvious answer, Jesus goes to another matter. He starts observing how the dinner guests are seeking out for themselves the best seats at the table. So, he calls for their attention and invites them always to take the humblest place.

> "When someone invites you to a wedding celebration, don't take your seat in the place of honor. Someone more highly regarded than you could have been invited by your host. The host who invited both of you would come and say to you,

'Give your seat to this other person.' Embarrassed, you would take your seat in the least important place. Instead, when you receive an invitation, go and sit in the least important place. When your host approaches you, he will say, 'Friend, move up here to a better seat.' Then you will be honored in the presence of all your fellow guests" (Luke 14:8-10).

Jesus loved to use stories of dinners and dinner invitations to teach important truths about the kingdom of God. There is an intimacy about sitting down together for a meal, something we are prone to lose with our fast-food culture and eating on the run. There is something holy about relaxing and sharing the same meal with others. The 'love feasts' of the early church were feasts of fellowship with Christ and one another. Most of us love to share meals with family, friends, and fellow Christians. But the next teaching of Jesus issues a command that goes far beyond the question of our place at the dinner table. In fact, it goes to the very heart of the gospel. It goes to *who we invite*, and that designation is a shocker.

Looking straight at the host of the wedding celebration, he says, "When you host a lunch or dinner, don't invite your friends, your brothers and sisters, your relatives, or rich neighbors … Instead, … invite the poor, crippled, lame, and blind" (14:12-13). I doubt that he's telling them never to invite the first group to a meal. Family and friends are not there for us to ignore. They are there for us to love. But there is another kingdom meal we are called to host or attend.

In a way, Jesus is teasing the host. He is suggesting something that the host has probably never considered, and Jesus knows it. We do not even know if the host—or anyone else at the banquet, for that matter—ever does host such a meal because of Jesus' call to do so. Not so hidden in Jesus' teaching is fallen humanity's addiction to a more civilized form of self-centeredness, to what we today call transactional relationships: I'll do something for you (like invite you to my banquet) because I know you will in turn do something for me (like invite me to your banquet). Jesus is inviting them to try something different, something not premised on a "what's in it for me." Doing something that is a giving, without expectation of a return.

"And you will be *blessed* because they can't repay you" (v. 14a, italics added). Blessed because they can't do anything for you. At a deeper level, however, they can do a lot for us. Jesus puts it this way: "Instead, you will be repaid when the just are resurrected" (v. 14b). In other words, inviting those who we previously thought were not our kind or socially beneath us will open our hearts to those who have much to teach us. Our reward will be a greater suitability for the feast of eternity for all who have gathered at the kingdom's diversity table, humbled like us.

Blessed, indeed, are the open table hosts!

> *Dear Jesus, as you have invited a sinner like me to the table of your gracious bounty, help me to follow suite with those I invite to my table. I ask in your name. Amen.*

JULY 28

THE FAVORED HUMBLE

Scripture for Reflection: Luke 1:46-49

These verses are part of one of the most extraordinary passages of the Gospels. Mary, the mother-to-be of Christ, is singing her own hymn of praise to the God who seems to have by-passed more prominent women to choose her, a little-known teenager of lowly status, to bear and birth the Messiah.

God has a strange tendency to honor the un-honored. To bless the humble. To favor the obscure, the skipped-over. To choose those deemed unlikely by our human standards. Like Mary.

In the Bible there are stories of God's intervening on behalf of women who are unable to bear children. Who can forget Sarah at ninety-nine years and Abraham at one hundred, being informed by three God-sent visitors that they will become pregnant? Abraham is incredulous and Sarah laughs, but Isaac comes along nine months later. Leah is not loved by her husband and does not bear children for seven years. Jacob then takes Rachel as his second wife and loves her more than Leah. Seeing that Leah is unloved, God has compassion on her and "opens her womb" so that she has four sons in succession. The First Book of Samuel begins with the story of Hannah, one of two wives married to Elkanah. The other wife is Peninnah. She is able to bear children and Hannah is not. Elkanah loves Hannah, and they both grieve over her barrenness, while Peninnah makes fun of her. Hannah implores God to give her a son. She promises God that if he gives her a son, she will give him to the Lord for the priesthood. The priest Eli gives her his blessing, the Lord gives her a son, and she in turn honors her promise. And there is Elizabeth, Mary's cousin, barren and now "too old" to have children. She, too, has miraculously become pregnant and will bear John the Baptist, forerunner of Jesus.

All these women were of humble status or recipients of scorn or devoid of hope for bearing a child. All of them caught God's eye. What was there about them that put them in his sights? Sara's inability to have children threatened the promise to Abraham. Leah and Hannah were disdained, Leah by Rachel and Hannah by Peninnah. Elizabeth bore the embarrassment and pity of the barren wives, who at that time were considered to have failed their purpose as wives. All we know about Mary is that she, a teenager, considered herself to be of low status and not highly favored—that is, until she was visited by an angel! The angel stunned her with these words: "Rejoice, favored one! The Lord is with you!" (Luke 1:28). This confused the teenager. The angel clarified:

> "'God is honoring you. Look! You will conceive and give birth to a son, and you will name him Jesus. He will be great and he will be called the Son of the Most High. The Lord will give him the throne of David his father.... There will be no end to his kingdom.... The Holy Spirit will come over you and the power of the Most High will overshadow you. Therefore, the one who is to be born will be holy. He will be called God's Son....' Then Mary said, 'I am the Lord's servant. Let it be with me just as you have said'" (Luke 1:30-37).

RENEWALS

The gospel begins with God's choice of a humble teenager to bear and raise the Messiah. It is then propelled forward by her faith and humility. The scope of it is sung in her Magnificat. The fulfilment of it is "mercy for everyone who honors him as God" (v. 50).

What are we to make of these miraculous interventions of God in the lives of women? At a time and in a society of male domination, here we see God deeply moved by the suffering of women who are unable to fulfill their role of bearing children. He takes action. He restores to them the dignity of child-bearing that in those days was so important. He sees women who are humbled by their childlessness. Genuine humility always draws his attention.

Mary knows her place: She confesses her "low status." This is no fake humility. She has had few privileges. She knows her place in the world of that day. But there is something about her that draws God. Is it her lack of presumption? The purity of her soul? The knowledge that she will see nothing about the recognition God is about to give her as in any way something she deserves? All we can say for sure is that this self-confessed servant of low estate (her words) has become, in the hands of God's own choosing, someone who will be "blessed."

Mary has something to teach the rest of us: Whatever status we hold in this world, God is not impressed. Only the humble will be favored (blessed), and the arrogant will fall.

Dear Lord, humble me so that I can be my true self and among those you bless. Amen.

JULY 29

THOSE WHO DIE IN THE LORD

Scripture for Reflection: Revelation 14:13 (NRSV)

Revelation seems most likely to have been written during the reign of the emperor Domitian (A.D. 81-96), who came to demand that his subjects address him as 'Lord and God' and worship his image. Faithful Christians, of course, could not do so, and they paid the price. They were either martyred or subjected to ongoing persecution and ostracization. Others left the church.

It was not the words of Jesus or an apostle, but "a voice from heaven" that announced a blessing of those who "die in the Lord." Heaven could see the cruelty its earthly citizens were subjected to. The gospel had won the hearts and lives of many in Asia Minor. Domitian, however, saw the threat not only to the divine authority he claimed but also to the stability of Roman rule in this key part of his empire. His persecutions were launched with a vengeance.

The apostle Paul had declared years earlier that the dead in Christ would rise at the final resurrection (1 Thessalonians 4:16). Now, the voice from heaven is specifically aimed at the followers of Jesus "who keep God's commandments and keep faith with Jesus" (Revelation 14:12). Earlier, John had seen in his vision "under the altar those who had been slaughtered on account of the word of God and the witness they had given" (6:9). Now the voice addresses all faithful Christians "who die in the Lord from here on" (14:13a).

Do all truly faithful Christians suffer persecution? The truth is that within two or three centuries following Domitian's reign, the church grew so large that beginning with Emperor Constantine, she became the state church of the empire and later, for most of the emerging European nations. Who, then, were the martyrs? They were the Christians who separated from the state churches and pursued a different and more radical understanding of Christian practice. They were also some of the missionaries from European and American churches who were attacked by members of other religions who saw Christianity as a threat to their own beliefs.

What about all other Christians who are not under such threats? I want to suggest that in our day they are under two threats that are more insidious. The threats are *dilution* and *dismissal*. The diluters of Christian faith are those who identify as Christians and at the same time live by the values of an excessively self-centered culture. It is an incompatible marriage. There is nothing about the Christian faith that allows for such compromise. One observer has concluded that most Christians today seem to worship more than one God. To be sure, it is difficult for most of us to shed the influences of the culture around us all at once. The good news is that over time the Spirit can help us identify those compromises, receive the grace of God's forgiveness, and begin afresh.

The other threat is the prevailing dismissal of one Christian group by another. This is not new, but today it seems excessively poisonous. The malignancy is multiplied by the identification of

Christian groups with specific political parties or movements, leading to the judgment that those in other political parties cannot possibly be Christians. The dismissal of Christians by other Christians has become a self-inflicted wound on the Body of Christ that calls for repentance.

Christians need to remind themselves that their deeds follow them. How they treat one another, including those Christians with political views different from their own, will either honor or demean the Body of Christ. It is one thing for Christians to debate politics; it is another for them to use political affiliation to question the authenticity of another Christian's faith.

The persecutions of Christians come both from those who do not profess Christian faith and from those who do. Which is *your* greater personal challenge? Which may be keeping you from being among those who die in the Lord, those who can happily rest from their labors because their deeds follow from strong faith and inclusive love?

> *Dear Lord, please give me the spiritual strength to meet the attacks of both enemies of Christ and Christians who dismiss me as a misguided follower of Jesus. Give me the grace to respond to both attacks, if they come, with Christly love and humility. I ask in the name of Jesus, who loved and took seriously everyone he met. Amen.*

JULY 30

THE BLESSED HOPE

Scripture for Reflection: Titus 2:11-16

This whole passage begins with a proclamation that appears in these words only here in the New Testament: "The grace of God has appeared, bringing salvation to all people." (v. 11). It is a powerful statement about the incarnation of Christ making possible a universal salvation. Once Christ accomplishes this through his death and resurrection, his church then awaits his return.

Some of us are not good waiters. We want tomorrow to be now. Disciples of Jesus, however, are called to be waiters when it comes to Jesus' glorious appearance to call us home. We cannot conjure up Jesus' return. We must wait. Wait because the gospel is for "all people." *All people!* If it's available for everyone, we've a long way to go in spreading the Word. Verse 12 tells us that saving grace instructs us so that we can begin to live "sensible, ethical, and godly lives right now by rejecting ungodly lives and the desires of this world." We wait for Jesus' return, not by sitting idly by, but by spreading his name and living his life in credible ways. Otherwise, we are just hoping, not *living in the hope* as Jesus calls us to do.

Paul is writing this letter to a trusted associate, Titus, a pagan convert mentored by Paul and now bishop of the church in Crete. He is advising Titus on some challenging issues that threaten to mislead or divide his flock. In giving him practical advice about his leadership, Paul reminds him that his ministry takes place in the flow of eternity: We are waiting for "the blessed hope and the glorious appearance of our great God and savior Jesus" (Titus 2:13). Jesus himself *is* the hope. He is the prize and the giver of eternal gifts. He said to his disciples that "the Son of Man is to come with his angels in the glory of the Father, and then he will repay everyone for what has been done" (Matthew 16:27, NRSV). Paul told the church in Rome, "We are saved in hope. If we see what we hope for, that isn't hope" (Romans 8:24). In other words, hope requires faith. Faith is the path we travel to who and what we hope for. To the Galatian church he said, "We eagerly wait for the hope of righteousness through the Spirit by faith" (Galatians 5:5). To the Colossian church he said, "You have this faith [in Christ Jesus] and love [for all God's people] because of the hope reserved for you in heaven" (Colossians 1:5a).

These references to hope are not so much about our hoping as they are about the One in whom we place our hope, the One who is the center of our hope, the One who is Hope-in-Person. Yes, Jesus, the One who "gave himself to us in order to rescue us from every kind of lawless behavior and cleanse a special people for himself who are eager to do good actions" (Titus 2:14). It is Jesus we wait for. He is our treasure, our Lord, our eternal life. The good acts we do are enabled by him and done for him. They anticipate how we will live together in communion with him and with our eternal family. This is the blessed hope we live every day until it is consummated in the resurrection, and hope becomes eternal life.

The New Testament gives witness to two appearings of

Christ. The first was the forty days during which the resurrected Christ appeared to his disciples, confirming his victory over death, reminding them of what he had taught them about the kingdom of God, and telling them to wait in Jerusalem for a baptism with the Holy Spirit (Acts 1:1-5). The second appearing, often referred to as 'the Second Coming,' is yet to come. Here it is described as "the blessed hope" and "the glorious appearance of our great God and savior Jesus Christ" (Titus 2:13). Christ will return in his full identity as God and his self-giving work as Savior.

"Talk about these things," says Paul to Titus. "Encourage and correct with complete authority. Don't let anyone disrespect you" (Titus 2:15). He is saying it to us as well. We, all of us, are the priesthood of believers. With love, we keep each other straight. With humility, we allow others to keep us straight. And all of us together are richly blest in our anticipation of "the glorious appearance of our great God and savior Jesus Christ."

> *Dear Christ, Hope of the world, forever blessing us with promises of eternal life, help me through your Spirit to live today in a way that gives a taste of your love and a hint of heaven's joy. I ask in your name. Amen.*

JULY 31

THOSE BLESSED BY THE FATHER, WELCOMED BY CHRIST

Scripture for Reflection: Matthew 25:31-46

These words of Jesus, appearing only in Matthew's Gospel, are the last of a series of his teachings about the return of Christ and the final judgment. The earlier teachings deal with the return of the Son of Man, the eternal endurance of his words, the unpredictability of the time of the return, the importance of being ready for his return, and the reward for those whose lives are invested in the Kingdom of Heaven.

The last teaching differs significantly from the others. It pictures the Son of Man sitting on his throne of glory, and all the nations are gathered before him. He is separating people into two groups, like a shepherd separates his sheep from his goats. One group is on his right, the other on his left. First, he summons those on his right to come, and he tells them they are "blessed by my Father" (Matthew 25:34, NRSV) and invites them to come and inherit the kingdom prepared for them. And then he tells them why they are invited. It is as simple as it is startling:

> "I was hungry and you gave me food to eat. I was thirsty and you gave me a drink. I was a stranger and you welcomed me. I was naked and you gave me

clothes to wear. I was sick and you took care of me. I was in prison and you visited me" (vv. 35-36).

When? When, Lord, did we see you in such needy situations? We don't remember. Tell us when! Their response is a beautifully poignant part of the story. These Kingdom-inheritors may have been able to remember a few times when they helped some of "the least of these," but they didn't consciously do it to get eternity points from Jesus. They weren't building some case for themselves, a portfolio of good works to gain entrance at heaven's gate. They were sharing compassion. Period. And yes, Jesus was there, hidden, remembering—not as an observer, but in the hunger, the thirst, the alienation, the nakedness, the sickness, and the imprisonment of the least. Jesus was seeing, feeling, experiencing it all. And he saw the holy love, the love that wants no return, save perhaps the sheer joy of it and a growing feeling that this is a huge part of what God made us for. Then the Lord replied to them, "I assure you that when you have done it for one of the least of these brothers and sisters of mine, you have done it for me" (v. 40).

The sad part of the story has to do with the other group Jesus addresses. This group is as clueless as the first group. But they are not clueless about their own acts of compassion, as the first group was. They are clueless about their own acts of uncaring, their insensitivity to the suffering of fellow human beings. They probably dismiss these sufferers as somehow deserving of misfortune and undeserving of human compassion. They have no use for "the least of these" and certainly entertain no suspicion of a divine calling to treat them with compassion. Some of them may have a religion of sorts, a religion with a god who "rewards those who help themselves," even at the expense of others. They see God present in successful people perhaps, but certainly not in "the least of these." They mistake who God is, and they refuse to be and do what the Jesus of the Gospels asks of them.

Unlike the previous parables of the Judgment, the accountability is not so clearly defined. Both groups—those who did well and those who didn't—are surprised that they have done, or not done, what Jesus is describing. Jesus is not making a judgment on how well they have followed a clear commission he's previously given to see him in "the least of these." He is revealing their hearts by comparison with his own. Jesus, whose heart is with and for those who are suffering and considered the least, has little time for those who hide behind their own sufficiency and success to shield them from those who suffer.

Why does Jesus spring this surprise on a day of Judgment? Perhaps there's something to be said for a genuine purity of heart, for doing something beautiful with no ulterior motive, with no motivation to impress God with an award-winning performance. Forced righteousness is not righteousness; transactional holiness is not holiness; and purity of heart is not something earned, it is a gift given to the truly humble.

No wonder both groups don't know. The one group doesn't know Jesus is present in "the least," so they continue to ignore them or exploit them. If they know, they might just give a little but keep themselves at a safe distance. The other group doesn't know either, so they love and help "the least" because they know Jesus does and because Christlikeness is their passion. Jesus puts himself in the parable as the hidden recipient of compassion. Who knows where else he hides himself? He probably hides himself in the privileged, calling his disciples to invite them to find the deeper joy of giving away, humbling themselves before God and serving "the least of these."

This parable invites us all to live as if Jesus is in or hanging around everyone, waiting for us to act like him, be like him, and see him calling out to us in the other, and especially in "the least."

If you're like me, you've still a way to go.

Dear everywhere-present Jesus, please cure me of any self-concern that blunts my awareness of those around me wherever I may be. Give me a keen eye for "the least of these," whether their least-ness is found in their hunger, thirst, alienation, nakedness, sickness, or imprisonment, or in the least-ness of a compassion deficit. Help me to get so used to doing so that I don't really know I am. I ask in your name, Jesus, Compassion in Person. Amen.

ADDENDUM
The Name of the First Person in the Trinity

Some Christians have expressed concern over the use of 'Father' to the exclusion of 'Mother' in the naming of the first Person. The use of 'Son' seems not to be as concerning, as the Christ became incarnate in the man Jesus. The male dominance of the family unit and in society at large during both Old and New Testament times would hardly have allowed for God to be seen specifically as a female. Seeing God as a male figure reflected cultural norms of male privilege. In such a climate, it is all the more extraordinary that the apostle Paul would say that in Christ there is neither male nor female (Galatians 3:28); and a thorough reading of Scripture will show how the actions and roles of women (beyond childbearing) were incredibly crucial in fulfilling God's plan. Nevertheless, throughout the course of the church's history, time and again women have been underestimated and devalued because of their gender.

In our time, this has begun to change, and that movement will continue. Sadly, some churches oppose it and have consequently alienated women who have either left their connection with faith communities or joined churches who respect their callings beyond "traditional roles." My own church, The Salvation Army, early on in its life (latter nineteenth century) defied the opposition to women in church leadership and appointed women to leadership roles, which the Body of Christ at large did not allow at that time. Even so, at times and in certain places around the world, the church has not practiced the inclusion of women's leadership and still needs to continue to hold itself accountable for gender inclusion.

Another issue in identifying the first Person in the Trinity as 'Father' relates to the actual experiences people have had with their own fathers. Consider those who were raised by those we would call "good parents"—a father and a mother. "Good parenting" usually refers to the idea that *both* the father and the mother gave their unique gifts to the child. Speaking personally, I can say that each of my parents gave me certain gifts the other could not. Furthermore, some of the gifts my mother gave me correspond to what the Bible says God gives his children. There is a feminine side to God that the image 'Father God' alone does not evoke.

Now consider the single-parent family. If the single parent is a woman, and especially if the father abandoned the family or was kicked out because of domestic abuse toward the mother or child, the image of a father is one of abandonment and cruelty for the child. If the father is present and continuing his cruel treatment, the impression on the child is probably worse and the damage more long-range. If the mother is kind and helpful to her children, the image of a God who is Father and not Mother is problematic. If the single mother does the best job possible in being both father and mother, then the male Father image of God is lost on the children, unless a kind and helpful male relative, for example, steps in and becomes a surrogate father.

Because of the gender limitations that come with the role of the father in our culture, and the baggage of control and cruelty that for many comes with the Father image in reference to God, some Christians have suggested that the Person of the Godhead we call the Father be called, instead, the *Parent*. Not Father God, but Parent God. This does help with the insufficient inclusion of mother-gifts in the divine image, and it does allow for separation from experiences of cruelty by fathers, and in some cases mothers. Some feminist Christians have suggested that 'Mother God' be used to bring out the mothering side of God when appropriate; others may have decided to use it in place of Father God.

In this book, I have chosen to remain with the designation of the first Person in the Trinity as the divine Father. Parent God sounds too impersonal and abstract. Mother God sounds like a god of pagan religions, most of which had their female gods. But while I continue to refer to 'God the Father,' I do so keeping in mind the mothering heart of God and the mothering skills that God so richly displays in his dealings with us.

And by the way, while God created man and woman, he is neither. It seems that his creation of *both* man and woman is how he reveals the image of God on earth. Both participate in the Fall, in redemption, and in the embodiment of the true image of God.

Works Cited

Bauerschmidt, Frederick C. *The Love that Is God: An Invitation to Christian Faith*. W.B. Eerdmans Publishing Co., 2020.

Doerr, Harriet. *Stones for Ibarra*. Penguin Books, 1985.

Muggeridge, Malcolm. *Something Beautiful for God: Mother Teresa of Calcutta*. New York, NY: Harper and Row, 1971.

Nouwen, Henri. *The Way of the Heart*. New York, NY: The Seabury Press, 1981.

Wilder, Thornton. *The Bridge of San Luis Rey*. HarperPerennial, 1955.